WORLD SERIES OF POKER
♦ ♠ ♥ ♣

P9-DDV-954

NO-LIMIT TOURNAMENT
★ HOLD'EM

OFFICIAL WORLD SERIES OF POKER® STRATEGY GUIDE

NO-LIMIT TOURNAMENT ★ HOLD'EM

AVERY CARDOZA

CARDOZA PUBLISHING

FREE ONLINE POKER MAGAZINE!
www.cardozabooks.com

Sign up now to read all about the exciting world of poker. Our online magazine is packed with tips, expert strategies, tournament schedules and results, gossip, news, contests, polls, exclusive discounts on hotels, prepublication book discounts, and words of wisdom from the world's top experts and authorities.

Cardoza Publishing is the foremost gaming publisher in the world with a library of more than 200 up-to-date and easy-to-read books and strategies. These authoritative works are written by the top experts in their fields and with more than 10,000,000 books in print, represent the most popular gaming books anywhere.

Acknowledgements
We thank the following individuals for their contributions: Seth Palansky, Jack Effel, Daniel Vogel, Elizabeth Anne Hill, Ty Stewart and Doyle Brunson.

ISBN 10:   1-58042-246-2
ISBN 13: 978-1-58042-246-8
Library of Congress Control Number: 2010921138
Front cover photo of money by Rob Gracie/GreasieWheels.com

Visit our website or write for a full list of products

CARDOZA PUBLISHING
P. O. Box 98115, Las Vegas, NV 89193
Toll-Free Phone (800)577-WINS
email: cardozabooks@aol.com
www.cardozabooks.com

TABLE OF CONTENTS

PART 3

WINNING NO-LIMIT HOLD'EM TOURNAMENT STRATEGY 107

PART 4

LOOKING BACK AT THE WSOP: 40+ YEARS OF EXCITING GROWTH AND GOLD BRACELETS   193

PART 5

HOLD'EM GLOSSARY   207

LIST OF TABLES

# INTRODUCTION

Imagine playing your way through thousands of opponents at a World Series of Poker event, getting to the final table, and then winning it all! It's not just the money, which is often over $1 million—or many, many millions if you win the *big one*—it's the prestige of winning a gold bracelet. Of being immortalized as a World Champion. That's every poker player's dream. Chances are it's your dream too. Fame, fortune, and your place in history!

Well, that dream can come true! As every champion admits, it takes some luck to go all the way, but don't be fooled—it takes a lot of skill as well.

In this book, the first-ever official World Series of Poker guide to winning the no-limit hold'em tournaments at the WSOP, we show you how to go deep in the big events and put yourself in position to win the championship. Not only will you learn how to win chips, you'll know how to survive on a short stack or use your big stack as a weapon to earn even more chips. We'll go over everything you need to do to compete and win in the World Series of Poker, from the basics of play and tournament rules, to the payout structures, to the best strategies for all four stages of a tournament.

You'll also learn how to play position, read players and take advantage of their tendencies, as well as how to bet and think at every stage of a hand—preflop, flop, turn and the river. You'll find out how to enter and win satellites and megasatellites so that you can earn entry into the WSOP tournaments for a fraction of the buy-ins. We'll also show you how to attack a hand, when to underbet, overbet, bet the pot, or use the hammer, the all-in bet!

A gold bracelet may be waiting for you, so let's get to it!

Part 1

NO-LIMIT HOLD'EM: POKER'S MOST EXCITING GAME

The thrill of playing no-limit hold'em comes partly from being able to bet all your chips on a single play. But of course, knowing when to go all-in comes from knowledge and experience. If you already know the basics of play, you can skip Chapter 1, which is devoted to readers who have never before entered the battle of wits it takes to win at poker's most exciting game. Move right along to Chapter 2, where you'll learn the seven keys that will open the door to success in no-limit hold'em cash games and tournaments.

 # THE MECHANICS OF NO-LIMIT HOLD'EM

OVERVIEW

Texas hold'em, or **hold'em**, as the game is more commonly known, is played as high poker; that is, the player with the best and highest five card combination at the showdown will have the winning hand and collect the money in the pot. The pot can also be won by a player when all of his opponents fold their hands at any point before the showdown, leaving one player alone to claim the pot—even though he may not actually have held the best hand!

Your final five-card hand in hold'em will be made up of the best five-card combination of the seven total cards available to you. These include the **board**, five cards dealt face-up in the middle of the table, cards which are shared by all players, and your **pocket cards** or **hole cards**, two cards dealt face-down that can be used by you alone. For example, your final hand could be composed of your two pocket cards and three cards from the board, one pocket card and four from the board, or simply all five board cards.

At the beginning of a hand, each player is dealt two face-down cards. Then each player gets a chance to exercise his betting options. Next, three cards are dealt simultaneously on the table for all players to share. This is called the **flop**, and it is followed by another round of betting. A fourth board card, called the **turn**, is then dealt, and it too is followed by a round of betting. One final community card is dealt in the center of the table, making five total. This is the **river**. If two or more players remain in the hand, it is followed by the fourth and final betting round.

When all bets have concluded, there is the **showdown**, in which the highest ranking hand in play wins the **pot**—the accumulation of bets that are kept in the center of the table. The pot can also be won by a player when all of his opponents fold their hands at any point before the showdown, leaving one player alone to claim the pot—even though he may not actually have held the best hand!

NO-LIMIT

No-limit hold'em is the exciting no-holds barred style of poker played in the World Series of Poker Main Event, and many of the preliminary tournaments that are part of the fifty-plus event WSOP schedule each year. The prevailing feature of no-limit hold'em, and what makes the game so exciting, is that you can bet any amount up to what you have in front of you on the table *anytime* it is your turn. That exciting "all-in" call signals a player's intention to put all his chips on the line.

THE BUTTON AND THE BLINDS

All play and strategy in hold'em depends upon the position of the **button**, a small plastic disk labeled "Dealer." The button designates the position from which the cards will be dealt. Actually, a casino employee deals the cards starting with the first player to the left of the dealer button. The player with the button in front of him, who is also known as the button, will have the advantage of acting last in every round of betting except for the preflop round. After each hand is completed, the disk rotates clockwise to the next player.

The player immediately to the left of the button is called the **small blind** and the one to his left is called the **big blind**. These two players are required to post bets, called **blinds**, before the cards are dealt.

In no-limit cash games, the amounts of the blinds are preset and remain constant throughout the game. Typical blinds for cash games might be $2/$5, $3/$5 or $5/$10 for the small blind and big blind respectively. Bigger blinds mean more action and larger games.

In tournaments, however, the blinds steadily increase as the event progresses, forcing players to play boldly to keep up with the greater costs of these bets. You'll learn how to adjust for this unique facet of tournament play in Part Three.

ANTES

Antes are mandatory bets that every player must make before the cards are dealt and are in addition to the blinds. They are only required in tournaments after some rounds, usually two or three, have been played.

SEATING ARRANGEMENTS

Around a poker table, Seat 1 identifies the place to the immediate left of the dealer, Seat 2 the chair to that player's left, and so on until Seat 10, which would be immediately to the right of the dealer in a 10-player game. While players can be identified in relation to where the dealer sits, a player's *position* has an entirely different meaning.

Position describes a player's relative position to the player acting last in a poker round. Thus, if the player in seat 5 is to bet first, he is in early position, and the player to his immediate right, who will act last since the action goes clockwise, will be in late position.

HAND RANKINGS

The standard poker rankings are used in hold'em. The royal flush is the highest, then the straight flush, four of a kind, full house, flush, straight, three of a kind, two pair, one pair, and then high card. The order in which cards are dealt or how they are displayed is irrelevant to the final value of the hand. For example, 7-7-K-A-5 is equivalent to A-K-7-7-5.

BETTING OPTIONS

When it is your turn to play, the following options, which apply to all forms of poker, are available to you:

1. **Bet**: Place a wager if no player has done so before it is your turn to act.
2. **Call**: Match a bet if one has been placed before your turn.
3. **Raise**: Increase the size of a current bet such that opponents, including the original bettor, must put additional money into the pot to stay active in a hand.
4. **Fold**: Give up your cards and opt out of play if a bet is due and you do not wish to match it. This forfeits your chance of competing for the pot.
5. **Check**: Stay active in a hand without making a bet and risking chips. This is only possible if no bets have been made.

The first three options—bet, call, and raise—are all a form of putting chips at risk in hopes of winning the pot. Once chips are bet and due, you must match that bet to continue playing for the pot or you must fold. Checking is not an option. If no chips are due, you can stay active in the hand without cost by checking.

If a bet has been made, each **active player**—one who has not folded—is faced with the same options: call, fold, or raise.

When a bet has been made, it no longer belongs to the bettor; it becomes the property of the pot, the communal collection of money that is up for grabs by all active players.

Betting continues in a round until the last bet or raise is called by all active players—or if all players have checked—at which point the betting round is over. A player may not raise his own bet when his betting turn comes around. He may raise only another player's bet or raise.

THE SHOWDOWN

If two or more players remain at the conclusion of all betting in the final betting round of a poker game, the showdown occurs. The **showdown** is the final act in a poker game where remaining players reveal their hands to determine the winner of the pot.

The player whose last bet or raise was called—or if all players checked, then the first to the left of the dealer position—turns over his cards first and reveals his hand. The player with the best hand at the showdown wins all the money in the pot. Players holding losing hands at the showdown may concede the pot without showing their cards.

In the event of a tie, the pot will be split evenly among the winners.

If only one player remains after the final betting round, or at any point during the game, there is no showdown. The remaining player automatically wins the pot and gets to collect all the chips.

THE ORDER OF BETTING

Play always proceeds clockwise around the table. On the preflop, the first betting round, the first player to the left of the big blind goes first. He can call the big blind to stay in competition for the pot, raise, or fold. Every player following him has the same choices: call, raise, or fold.

The last player to act on the preflop is the big blind. If no raises have preceded his turn, the big blind can either end the betting in the round by calling—no further chips need to be put in since his blind bet has already been made—or he can put in a raise. However, if there are any raises in the round, the big blind and other remaining players must call or raise these bets to stay active, or they must fold.

On the other betting rounds—the flop, turn and river—the first active player to the button's left will go first and the player on the button will go last. If the button has folded, the player sitting closest to his right will act last. When all bets and raises have been met on the flop and turn, or if all players check, then the next card will be dealt. On the river, after all betting action is completed, players will reveal their cards to see who has the best hand.

Betting in a round stops when the last bet or raise has been called and no bets or raises are due any player. Players cannot raise their own bets or raises.

At any time before the showdown, if all opponents fold, then the last active player wins the pot.

PLAYING TIP

Never fold in the big blind if no one has raised—unless you want to reraise. Otherwise, you can see the flop at no additional cost by simply tapping the table.

A SAMPLE GAME

If you've been playing limit poker, you already know that the betting structure has two levels, the lower levels being the amount you must bet or raise on the preflop and flop (for example, 3 in a 3/6 limit game), and the higher levels being the amount you must bet or raise on the turn and river (for example, 6 in a 3/6 limit game).

No-limit hold'em games proceed exactly like limit hold'em games—the same order of play and the same options are available to the players. The only difference is that there is no cap to the amount that you can bet. You can bet or raise any amount greater than the minimum allowed, up to all your chips, when it is your turn.

Before the cards are dealt, the small blind and the big blind must post their bets. Once that occurs, the dealer distributes cards one at a time, beginning with the small blind, who is the player sitting to the immediate left of the button, and proceeding clockwise until all players have received two cards face down.

Now let's take a look at how a 25/50 no-limit hold'em betting round works in a tournament with nine players around the table. (Note that a full-handed World Series of Poker hold'em tournament typically starts with ten-player tables, and later, as the field thins, they get reduced to nine-player tables.)

The Preflop

The player to the big blind's left acts first. He has the option of calling the 50 big blind bet, raising it, or folding. Checking is not an option on the preflop as there is already a bet on the table—the 50 big blind bet.

Let's say that the first player folds. The next player is faced with the same decisions: call, raise, or fold. He calls for 50. The next three players fold. The following player raises 100, making it 150 total—the 50 call plus the 100 raise. Now it is the button's turn, the player sitting in the dealer position. He thinks about his situation and calls the 150. The small blind is the next player to act. The small blind has already put in 25 so he must put in 125 more to play. If there had been no raise, it would cost him just 25 more to meet the 50 big blind bet and stay active—but that's not the case here.

The small blind folds and the big blind considers reraising the raiser, but instead just calls the 100 raise. Play now moves back to the original caller. Since he has only put 50 into the pot, he must meet the 100 raise to stay in the hand. He calls. Since all bets and raises have now been matched, the preflop round is over.

We'll see the flop four-handed: with the original caller, the raiser, the big blind, and the button.

Note that the big blind always has the option to raise on the preflop. If there had been no raises before the big blind's turn to act, then the dealer will ask the big blind if he wishes to raise by announcing "option." If the big blind just calls, the preflop betting is finished for the round. If the big blind exercises his option and raises, then the other active players must meet that raise to stay active.

If all players fold on the preflop, that is, there are no callers, then the big blind wins the hand by default.

The Flop

At the conclusion of betting, the dealer pulls the blinds and bets into the pot. He takes the top card off the deck and **burns** it, that is, he removes it from play, and then deals the three-card flop face-up in the center of the table.

Minimum bets during this round and the subsequent betting rounds must be at least the size of the big blind. Since the big blind is 50, no player may bet less than that. However, the game is no-limit, so a player may lead out the betting for any amount 50 or more—up to all his chips.

The first active player to the button's left goes first. Since the small blind has folded, it is the big blind's turn. There are no bets that have to be met—the forced first round blind bet only occurs on the preflop—so the big blind may check or bet. (However, there is no reason to fold—which would be foolish—no matter how bad his hand might be, as it costs nothing to stay active.)

The big blind checks, the original caller checks, the original raiser from the preflop checks, and it is now up to the button. He pushes out 300, about half the amount in the pot, forcing the other three players to put up 300 if they want to see another card. The big blind, who checked first in this round, is the next active player. He must call or raise this bet to continue with the hand, or he must fold. He decides to call the 300. The remaining two players toss their cards with disgust and fold. The flop, apparently, didn't help them enough, so they wisely got out of the way. Since all bets have been called, betting is complete for the round.

We're now heads-up, the big blind versus the button.

The Turn

The dealer burns the top card and then deals a fourth community card face-up on the table. This is known as the **turn** or **fourth street**. The big blind, being the first active player on the button's left, goes first and checks. He could have chosen to bet 50 instead, the minimum bet (the size of the big blind) or any amount greater than 50, up to all his chips. (A typical wager though, if you were to put chips into the pot, would be to bet half the pot up to the full amount of the pot.)

The button checks as well. Since all active players have checked, the betting round is over.

The River and the Showdown

After the top card is burned, the fifth and final community card is turned over and placed next to the other four cards in the center of the table. Players now have five community cards along with their two pocket cards to form their final five-card hand.

At the **river** or **fifth street**, there is one final round of betting. The big blind goes first and leads out with a 500 bet. The button calls, which concludes the betting since the big blind cannot raise his own bet. We now have the showdown. The big blind turns over K-Q, which combines with a board of K-Q-10-7-5 for two pair of kings and queens. The button's K-10 also gives him two pair led by kings, but his second pair is tens. The big blind has the superior hand and wins the money in the pot.

Had the button simply folded, the big blind would have won by default, since no other players remained to contest the pot.

On the showdown, the last player to bet or raise (or if there has been no betting in the round, then the first person to the left of the button) has to show his cards first. Losers can simply **muck** their cards, that is, fold them, without showing their hand.

The dealer pushes the chips in the pot over to the winner, collects and shuffles the cards, and prepares to deal a new hand. The button moves clockwise, as it will after the completion of each hand, so the big blind is now the small blind, and the small blind becomes the button.

READING THE FLOP

You only start with two cards in your hand, and your cards must connect with the board to form certain hands, like pairs, trips (slang for three of a kind), straights, flushes, and full houses. Below are examples that show how various types of hands can be formed from the flop.

1. THE FLOP: THREE SUITED CARDS

Biggest Possible Hand on This Flop: Flush

WHAT TO LOOK OUT FOR:

A flush can be made only if there are three suited cards on board. In this example, any player holding two diamonds would have a flush. If there were only two suited cards on board, no player could currently hold a made flush, though one could be formed later if a third flush card showed on board.

2. THE FLOP: TWO SUITED CARDS

Biggest Possible Hand on This Flop: Three of a Kind

WHAT TO LOOK OUT FOR:

This flop is identical to the one previous, except that the last card, the 7, is a club. When the flop contains two suited cards, you know that an opponent will need a third suited card to complete the flush. An opponent may be drawing to a flush, but he cannot make one unless another diamond falls on the turn or river.

3. THE FLOP: THREE CONSECUTIVE CARDS

Biggest Possible Hand on This Flop: Straight

WHAT TO LOOK OUT FOR:

Any player holding J-10, 6-5, or 10-6 has flopped a straight. There are also straight draws out there for any player holding any J, 10, 6, or 5 as one of their two cards. If you hold a pair of tens, this flop is excellent. You have an **overpair** (a higher pair than any board card) and a straight draw. However, if you have a premium pair such as aces or kings, this flop is terrible. You have to worry about opponents cracking them with straights and straight draws.

4. THE FLOP: PAIR ON BOARD

Biggest Possible Hand on This Flop: Four of a Kind

WHAT TO LOOK OUT FOR:

Once a pair forms on board, three of a kinds, full houses, and even quads are possible. Any player who holds K-J is seeing one of the prettiest flops he's ever seen (a full house of jacks and kings)—but that's not quite as pretty as it is to a player holding two pocket kings for a bigger full house or a player holding two jacks for quads!

5. THE FLOP: CONSECUTIVE CARDS—TWO GAP

Biggest Possible Hand on This Flop: Straight

WHAT TO LOOK OUT FOR:

When there are no more than two gaps between the cards on board, it is possible that a player has flopped a straight. In this example, a player holding a 10-9 as pocket cards loves what he's looking at. Other two-gap flops include J-10-7 and J-9-7. One-gap flops include J-10-8 and J-9-8. If the flop has more than two gaps between the cards, it is impossible for any player to have made a straight. Thus, no player can have a straight if the flop comes J-8-6 (two gaps between the 9 and 10, and one gap between the 8-6).

POSSIBLE HANDS FORMED BY THE BOARD	
Board Shows	**Possible Hands**
Three suited cards	Flush
Three consecutive cards (2 gaps or less)	Straight
Pair on board	Three of a kind, full house, or quads

HOW TO READ THE FLOP: THREE PRACTICE HANDS

See if you can figure out the types of hands that can be formed from the flops below. Answers and explanations are on the following pages.

FLOP ONE

FLOP TWO

FLOP THREE

ANSWERS: THREE PRACTICE HANDS

FLOP ONE

Best Hands by Rank	Player's Hole Cards
Straight flush spades	7♠ 6♠
Any flush	Any two spades with A♠ being the highest
Straight	7-6 in any suit, but not both spades
Three of a kind	9-9, 8-8, 5-5

Key Points:

A flop of three suited cards (spades, in this example) means that any player holding two spades as pocket cards has a made flush. Forming a completed flush on the flop is impossible unless all three cards are suited. A straight is also possible because there are less than two gaps between the cards, but that would be a dangerous hand to play given the flush possibilities on board. And note the straight-flush possibility!

FLOP TWO

Best Hands by Rank	Player's Hole Cards
Three of a kind	J-J, 10-10, 6-6
Two pair	J-10, J-6, 10-6,
Pair	A-A, K-K, Q-Q, jack-any

Key Points:

Without three suited cards on the board, no flush is possible. And with the flop being **rainbow**, all different suits, there is no flush draw to be concerned with. Neither is there a made straight draw, as the flop has more than two gaps. The best hand any player can currently hold is a set (three of a kind).

FLOP THREE

Best Hands by Rank	Player's Hole Cards
Four of a kind	Q-Q
Full house	Q-10, 10-10
Three of a kind	Q-x (x - any card other than a 10)
Two pair	A-A, K-K, 10-x (x- any card other than queen)

Key Points:

A pair on the board makes a full house possible, as well as a rare four-of-a-kind hand. Whenever a pair flops, it is impossible for any player to have made a completed flush or straight. In this example, a player with two clubs would have a flush draw, and a straight draw would be possible with any of these combinations: A-J, K-J, K-9, J-9, and J-8. These draws would need a good card to come on the turn or river to complete, but a player going for a straight should be concerned about a third club falling. And everyone on a draw knows that a full house is possible.

HOW TO READ THE BOARD: FOUR PLAYERS

In the following example, you will see all five board cards. See if you can figure out the best hand held by each player.

PLAYER A

PLAYER B

PLAYER C

PLAYER D

THE BOARD

THE MECHANICS OF NO-LIMIT HOLD'EM

ANSWERS: THE BEST HANDS, FOUR PLAYERS

The Hands Formed:

Player A   Two pair: aces and fives
                             A♠ A♦ 5♥ 5♦ K♠

Player B   Two pair: nines and fives
                             9♥ 9♦ 5♥ 5♦ J♥

Player C   Full house: fives full of aces
                             5♥ 5♦ 5♣ A♦ A♥

Player D   Flush: diamond flush
                             9♦ A♦ 5♦ 6♦ 7♦

The Best Hands

Going to the river, Player C was leading with two pair, aces and fives, but there was danger. Diamond and heart flush draws were possible, and Player C did not want to see either one of those suits come on the river card. And indeed, two players, Player B and Player D were on flush draws. In fact, Player D was on both a flush draw *and* an inside straight draw, needing any diamond to complete the flush and an 8 to make a straight. If that 8 was a diamond, the hand would be a monster—a straight flush! Player A picked up aces on the turn, but like Player C, had to feel nervous about those flush draws.

The river does bring another diamond, making a diamond flush possible. While Player A improves to two pair, aces and fives, he is doomed by the flush made by Player D. And Player B also makes two pair, but those fives, being on board, helped Player A much more as the aces and fives are stronger than the nines and fives. Player B would have preferred a heart to make the flush, but only as long as that heart didn't make a full house for an opponent!

Player D got his diamond, but a dangerous diamond it was. It paired the board, making a full house—a stronger hand—

WSOP: TOURNAMENT NO-LIMIT HOLD'EM   37

possible. And sure enough, Player C completes his full house, catching a beautiful 5♦ to take the pot.

SEVEN KEYS TO SUCCESS AT NO-LIMIT HOLD'EM

The following key concepts will open the doors to success at all forms of hold'em—and for that matter, all forms of poker. These keys are particularly important to winning at no-limit hold'em.

1. Read Your Opponents
2. Play Aggressively
3. Respect Position
4. Play Strong Starting Cards
5. Aim to Win Chips, Not Pots
6. Fold When You're Beat
7. Remain Patient

Now let's take a look at how each concept improves your results at the table, beginning with the two most important items.

1. READ YOUR OPPONENTS

Poker is a game of cards played against people. Or as some players say, a people game played with cards. How opponents react to your betting actions, and you to theirs, determines who is going to win and who is going to lose. In the long run, every player is going to get the same number of good cards and bad cards. But it is how you play the cards you're dealt that determines if you're going to walk away with more chips than you started. And how you play those cards is determined by the opponents you're playing against. To win, you must play your opponents strategically, adjusting to their strengths and taking advantage of their weaknesses.

By watching how an opponent plays, you get all sorts of information on how to take advantage of his tendencies. For example, when a player infrequently enters a pot, he's **tight**, and you can often force him out of hands by making bets and raises, even when he may have better cards than you. You'll give him credit for big hands when he's in a pot, and get out of his way unless you have a big hand yourself.

On the other hand, an opponent who plays a lot of hands is **loose**, and you can figure him for weaker cards on average. You also need to adjust for **aggressive** players, who often raise when they get involved in a pot, and **passive** players, who you can play against with less fear of getting raised.

Becoming a better poker player requires a lot of knowledge—but to a great degree, improving your game depends on reading your opponents better than they read you. When you understand the tendencies and playing styles of your opponents, you can formulate a plan on how to outmaneuver and defeat them.

Two important traits define a winning poker player. The first is an ability to read opponents. It is so important that I've devoted an entire chapter, *How to Predict the Actions of Your Opponents*, to a broader discussion on how you can adjust your strategies to take advantage of your opponents' tendencies and weaknesses.

The second trait is a running theme throughout this book. We'll turn to it now.

2. PLAY AGGRESSIVELY

The best hold'em players share one common trait—aggression. When they're in a hand, they put the action to their opponents by either betting when they act first or when an opponent checks to them, or raising when it's bet to them. They make their opponents make tough decisions. And if you want to elevate your game, you need to do the same.

Betting when no bets are due, and raising when you get there, puts pressure on your opponents and forces them to commit more chips in order to stay in competition for the pot. One big advantage of playing aggressively is that it often causes opponents to fold, giving you a "free" pot without having to face a showdown. When they fold, you have a 100 percent chance of winning—and you can't beat that with a stick. Aggressive play also allows you to narrow the field or isolate opponents.

Being heads-up gives you a much better shot of winning a pot than playing against three or more players. You have only one person to beat. If two opponents enter pots with hands of equal strength and play about the same way, you can expect that, with all other things equal, you have a fifty-fifty shot of winning. Of course, all other things will not always be equal. But in the long run, if you're heads-up and push at an opponent with another bet, your chances of winning increase because you increase the likelihood that he will fold and give up the pot. Aggressive play shifts the odds. The bettor or raiser is the favorite to win for exactly that reason.

As you can see, aggressive betting makes the math start to look better. Your opponents become more cautious, you get more free cards when you want them, your opponents fold more often when you bet, and they become more reluctant to lead out against you because they know you might raise them right back. Best of all, aggressive betting makes your opponents more predictable, giving you a clearer picture of how to proceed when they play back at you.

When you put pressure on opponents, it gives you the strength and your opponents the fear. Aggressive play lets you set the tempo of the game and forces opponents to play at *your* pace.

3. RESPECT POSITION

Where you sit relative to the button in hold'em is called your **position**. In a nine-handed game, the first three spots to the left of the button are known as **early position**, the next three, **middle position**, and the last three, **late position**. In a ten-handed game, early position is the four spots to the left of the button.

The later your position, the bigger your advantage, because you get to see what your opponents do before deciding whether to commit any chips to the pot. Position is extremely critical in hold'em because it is maintained for four betting rounds—the preflop, flop, turn and river. If you have later position than opponents, this advantage becomes a significant weapon that you can use to bully players who must act before you. Conversely, the earlier your position, the more vulnerable your hand is to being raised and thus the more powerful your hand must be for you to enter the pot.

For example, let's say that you just call the big blind from early position with a mediocre hand, hoping to get in cheap to see the flop. If an opponent raises and your hand is not strong enough to call, you have cost yourself chips. This is particularly true in no-limit and pot-limit games where the raise could be for a lot of chips. If you **limp** (you just call as opposed to raising) too often and are pushed out of pots by aggressive raisers, you'll lose lots of chips without getting the benefit of seeing additional cards for your bet.

Thus, position is a big factor when deciding whether you should play 2-2 or J-J, for example. Position is also a factor to consider in deciding whether you should bet, raise, or fold. In the long run, you'll play more hands and have better results from a late position than from a middle or early position because your advantage is greater the closer you are to the button. More options and leverage mean more success—more chips—and that's what position is all about.

Let's take the starting cards of K-Q. You're first to act in a no-limit game and you limp into the pot. A tight player sitting in a later position raises. (In poker parlance, he is sitting **behind** you.) If you call that raise, you're probably an underdog to a better hand, so you throw the cards away. You've just lost chips because you left yourself vulnerable in early position. If you keep playing vulnerable hands that can't stand raises from early position, you're going to lose too many chips. And if you defend weaker hands against raises, your chip losses will be even worse.

If you're in late position, it's a different story. You have more options and leverage, so you can play more hands. If the early betting action is aggressive, you can fold marginal hands without cost. And if the betting action is weak, you can be more aggressive with marginal hands and see the flop with better position. You can decide whether that K-Q is worth a further bet based upon seeing the action around the table before it gets to you. If there is a big raise before you (**in front** of you, in poker talk), you can throw your K-Q to the wind without any cost. And if you think the hand is worth some chips, you can enter the pot with less risk of being raised—and that makes a very big difference.

TIP

As a general rule in any form of hold'em, you need stronger hands to play up front and weaker hands from the back. For example, if all players have folded to you on the button, you can play weaker hands since the only threats of raises behind you are the two blinds— who, if they do play with you, will be out of position on the next three betting rounds.

---

4. PLAY STRONG STARTING CARDS

Starting out with good cards gives you the best chance of winning. While this may seem obvious, you'd be surprised at the number of players who ignore this basic strategic concept and take loss after loss by chasing with inferior and losing hands. If you play too many hands in poker, you'll soon find yourself without chips. Enter the pot with good starting cards in the right position and you'll have a good chance of finishing with winners.

Sometimes you're dealt playable starting cards—but more often, you're not. In the first case, you play the good hands and see where they take you. But in the second instance, where your cards are not promising and you're a big underdog, folding is the proper strategy.

You don't want to give away bets. The preflop is where you make the decision of whether or not to play the hand at all. If you decide to play, do you want to get in and see the flop cheaply? Or do you want to try to win the pot right on the spot with an intimidating bet? When you play no-limit, you'll notice a very curious thing: The majority of no-limit pots are won right on the preflop, when one player raises and everyone else folds, whereas in limit poker, multiple players often see the flop since the entry fee into the pot is smaller.

You can't win every hand. Don't even try. Be judicious with the hands you choose to play. Hands that start strong tend to end strong. Hands that start weak tend to end weak. Of course, strong hands may die on the vine, and weak ones can grow into big hands, but if you continually play speculative hands hoping you'll draw out with them, you're going to lose a lot of chips.

5. AIM TO WIN CHIPS, NOT POTS

Your goal is to win money, not pots. There is a significant difference between the two. After all, at the end of a poker session, you're not going to measure your results by how many pots you won, but by how much money you won or lost. Winning money is what counts in poker—the final result.

Many novice players have the misconception that winning more pots equates to being a bigger winner at the tables. In fact, the opposite is true! Aggressive weak players tend to win more pots than stronger players because they're playing too many hands. Naturally, the more hands you play to the end, the more hands you will win—but winning more hands doesn't necessarily lead to getting more chips. Every pot contested comes at a cost. When you contest many and lose many, you can end up having a mighty bad day. In a do or die tournament, where you can't buy more chips, that's not a good thing.

It is not the quantity of pots you win, but the quality of them that matters. When you've got a big hand, you want to extract as many chips from your opponents as you can. Many beginning players make the mistake of pushing opponents out of hands in which they could have extracted more chips by betting too high, forcing their opponents to immediately fold. This doesn't mean you should not aggressively bet your big hands. On the contrary, you need to protect hands that are strong by betting aggressively. But be aware that sometimes you can extract more chips from opponents by allowing them to see another card, or in no-limit, by making bets that opponents feel compelled to call, even though they think they've got the worst of it in a hand.

Of course, the problem with betting strong hands weakly, called **slowplaying**, is that you don't get big hands very often. If you're in a tournament, you may only see a situation like that once or twice in a day. Perhaps not at all. But in the meantime, you've got to earn chips by being aggressive in the right situations, and by baiting opponents into pots you're likely to win in others.

No matter how you play a hand, don't lose sight of the basic goal—winning chips.

6. FOLD WHEN YOU THINK YOU'RE BEATEN

This concept sounds so obvious at first glance, you might be thinking: "Duh, really?" The answer, "Yes, *really.*" Too often, in fact, all of the time, I see players dropping chips in pots at the World Series of Poker when they should be out of the hand. Winning money in poker is not just about winning pots. Being an overall winning player has more to do with losing *less* when your cards don't come than winning big when you have the best hand! Many players don't appreciate this concept. They might get dealt enough good hands and win enough pots, yet they can't understand why they keep leaving the table with losses or marginal wins.

Folding when you're beaten is one of the most important concepts in poker. For example, let's say you're dealt **A♦ A♥**, the best possible starting hand in hold'em. You bring it in for a raise from early position, and get two callers. On the flop, three spades fall and you have none. You bet, a second players raises, and then a third player reraises.

You're facing potential flushes, and given all this action, your pocket rockets may be a huge underdog. If you call, you might get reraised again, perhaps with an all-in bet. Either way, this is a potential going-home hand. And if a straight draw such as 7-8-9 falls, or a pair forms on board—particularly a high pair since opponents are more likely to hold high cards than low cards—and you don't have a piece of it, your aces may be up against trips.

Even if you you're playing aces heads-up, there are times you have to recognize that you may be beat because there is too much strength on the board and your opponent is betting aggressively. Sure, aces start strong, but once the flop falls, you always need to reevaluate their relative value.

ESSENTIAL CONCEPT

Making good folds in poker is as important as making good bets.

More money is lost by players who consistently make bet after bet in clearly losing situations than in possibly any other facet of poker. Every extra bet you contribute to an opponent's pot is one more bet gone from your stack. To be a winner at poker, you must hold your chips dear and value them as if they were gold. There are good bets in poker, and there are bad bets. If you can cut the number of your bad bets in half, you'll turn losing sessions into winning sessions and small winning sessions into larger winning sessions.

Do not play with cards that cannot win. Never lose sight of this concept when you're playing. When you lose, you should lose on hands you thought would be winners or which gave you good odds to play out as an underdog. Never lose with hands on which your odds of winning aren't worth the bets you're making; you shouldn't even be playing these cards.

Folding losing hands will earn you more chips at poker in the long run than any other strategic aspect of the game. In fact, it is *essential* if you're going to be a winning player. Getting rid of weak hands should not be interpreted as advice to play like a rock, exit pots just because your hand is a dog, or bet only when you're in the lead. Far from it. Smart poker play means balancing bets with your chances of winning, and that includes playing for pots when you're strong, when you're trailing, and sometimes—given the right pot odds or the right opponent—when you're weak.

Your goal in tournaments must be to win chips. Having constant action and being part of every pot will rapidly drain your bankroll. By definition, it means you're playing in too many pots, with too many inferior hands, for too long. This is not a winning strategy. Learning to recognize when you're beat or a big underdog in a situation will save you more chips than you can imagine.

7. REMAIN PATIENT

Hold'em is a game of patience. You will often endure long stretches between getting dealt good hands. Winning players remain calm and wait patiently for situations where they can win chips. Your good hands will come. If you haven't blown yourself out trying to force plays—and are still around with chips in your pile—you'll be able to take advantage of your good hands and win some nice pots for yourself. As the old saying goes, "You have to be in it, to win it." Too many players, itching to get some kind of action going, will stick their necks out with bets in inadvisable situations, and get their stacks chopped down to the felt.

Tournaments, even more than cash games, require patience. Lots of it. In a tournament, the first few rounds are all about waiting for opportunities. The blind and ante bets are minimal, so there is no hurry to force play. You have lots of time to wait for good situations to come your way. Many novices make the terrible mistake of pushing too hard, too early, when they have no reason to risk their tournament lives on foolish plays. When the blinds get high enough to hurt your stack, or when you think the right opportunity has come along, then it's time to play more aggressively. Otherwise, think of yourself as a lion on the hunt. Just sit and wait—the right prey will come along, sooner or later.

As you approach the money table in a World Series of Poker tournament, patience is more important than ever. You must wait for good situations, but not so long that you lose too much of your stack to the erosive march of the blinds. When an opportunity presents itself, strike hard and try to build some chips, because if you can hang around long enough, you'll get into the top 10 percent of all players in the tournament. And that means you'll get into the money! And that's when you can set your sights even higher.

Now that we've put the keys to success in our pocket, let's see how much they affect our strategies in no-limit hold'em games. The next part of this book goes into extensive detail on how to win no-limit hold'em tournaments at the World Series of Poker.

Let's get the game going!

Part 2

WINNING NO-LIMIT HOLD'EM STRATEGY

If you've got the guts to put all your chips on the line, no-limit hold'em is the game for you!

Your entire stack of chips is at risk on every single hand in no-limit action—as are those of your opponents. One big mistake and poof, your chips vanish like smoke in the wind. Goodbye chips, hello rail. In limit hold'em, one bet is only one limited bet, but no-limit hold'em, one bet could be all your chips. It might even be the defining moment of your game. And that changes everything.

In no-limit, you must tread carefully every step of the way. What if you bet 200 on the preflop, and your opponent raises you all-in?

Yikes! Now what do you do?

For a quick answer, you'd better have the goods, and I mean you *really* need to have the goods if all your chips are on the line. Otherwise, you'd better fold your hand and give up the pot. Do you really want all your chips committed to an inferior hand when you're barely getting your seat warmed up? Unless, of course, you're convinced your opponent doesn't hold as strong a hand as yours—but do you really want to take that big a risk?

Anyone can wave that big stick over another player. And that is what changes the nature of every bet and move you make in no-limit. I call this type of intimidating big bet, or just the threat of one, the **hammer**. You must adjust for the possibility that an opponent will use the hammer and move a massive number of chips into the pot against you. Or you might need to use the hammer yourself to intimidate an opponent. And that requires fearlessness, the fortitude to put your chips on the line. It also requires that you know when you should fold, because if you make a poor decision, you'll lose all your chips—never a fun ending.

In cash games, you're not worried too much about the blinds, because they're generally small, nor are you concerned with antes, because there aren't any. Your goal in a cash game is purely and simply to win chips. You don't care if you have more chips than other players, or less, as long as you finish with more of them than you started with. And then you have won money.

When you have a good session and win lots of chips, you can take them off the table and leave any time you want. The chips you play with can be converted to real profits whenever you choose. Not so with tournaments.

The basic strategies for no-limit hold'em that are detailed here in Part Two apply to tournaments, though they also can be used in cash games. As soon as you've mastered these basics, you will need to further tweak your game and adapt this basic strategy to more complex tournament situations. We show you how to do that in Part Three, *Tournament No-Limit Hold'em Strategy*.

WINNING STRATEGY BEFORE THE FLOP: ENTER OR EXIT?

The blinds have been posted, and the cards are in the air. The game is on! You look down at your two cards.

What to do?

You consider your options while your opponents watch your every move. You need a game plan and, if nothing else, there is one thing you do know: You want to go all the way. You're after that bracelet and the first-place prize money. But first, you have a hand to play and the decision is on you.

This chapter is all about how to make the best decisions before you see the flop.

THINKING BEFORE THE FLOP

If you want to be a successful no-limit hold'em player, you can't play a lot of hands. Most of the time, in fact, you'll fold hand after hand while you wait for either good hands or good situations before tossing chips to the middle of the felt. We talked about this earlier and we need to talk about it again now. No-limit hold'em is a game of patience. Your best strategy for getting deep into a tournament and putting yourself in position to win is to play few hands in the right positions, and play them strong. This style of play is commonly called **tight-aggressive**; *tight* because you play few hands, and *aggressive* because you bet and raise when you're in a pot, forcing opponents to play against a lot of pressure.

Top players can get away with playing very aggressively with a lot of hands because of their superior people-reading skills. They pick up a lot of small pots by forcing opponents out with bets and raises. These players are not playing their cards, they are playing their opponents. As you get comfortable with the dynamics of no-limit hold'em, you can open up and play more hands in more situations. But as an amateur player, playing a narrower range of hands—and playing them skillfully—will give you great opportunities to win money in the World Series of Poker no-limit hold'em tournaments.

The general guidelines in this section will help you decide when and how to enter the pot before the flop in no-limit hold'em. These basic strategies are often referred to as playing **A-B-C poker**. They are the backbone of a solid strategy and give you a sense of the right play to make most of the time. However, if you make these plays *all* of the time, you'll be predictable and way too easy to read at the table. The circumstances of your situation—the tenor of the game, the types of players you are up against, the texture of the flop, and the dynamics of the table—will affect how often you'll deviate from these general guidelines. In a tournament, your chip count and that of your opponents, how deep in the tournament you are, and the pressure of the blinds and antes are additional factors that affect how you play your hands.

No-limit hold'em is a situational game. While the starting cards you hold are important, four other factors strongly influence the proper course to take when it is your turn to act. For example, if you asked me how to play a pair of fives, my answer would be these four questions:

1. What is your position at the table?
2. What is your table image?

3. Did anyone bet in front of you? (What kind of player is this opponent?)
4. Is the table tight or loose? (What are the dynamics?)

If you were playing in a tournament, consider two additional questions:

- How many chips do you have compared to the big blind?
- How many chips do your opponents have compared to the big blind?

How you play pocket fives is like asking what you do with a pistol when an adversary faces you. It depends—it always depends. If your adversary is a tank or an army, I suggest you back off. If your adversary holds a butter knife and you show the gun and a willingness to use it, I'd suggest that your opponent should be the one to back down.

So what do you do when you have a pair of fives? *It depends.* As we go over the starting hands, we'll consider all the factors that influence your decision as to whether to commit chips to your starting hand or fold the cards and wait for a better situation.

Let's begin with early position.

Early Position

The best starting cards in no-limit hold'em are the **premium hands**—pocket aces, kings, queens, jacks, A-K, and A-Q. In an unraised pot, bring these hands in for a standard raise in early position. Your goal is to either win the pot right there when all players fold, or to narrow the field to one or two callers who will see the flop with you.

If you have A-A or K-K, hopefully you'll get a caller or two or, even better, a raiser. Then you'll raise or reraise the size of the pot, or go in for all your chips if you get reraised. With Q-Q and A-K, you can stand a raise to see the flop, but if the raise is for all your chips and you're not short-stacked, you may need to let these hands go. If you don't want your day finished off by pocket queens, you certainly don't want to go out with J-J or A-Q! If an opponent puts in a big raise or even goes all-in when you hold J-J or A-Q, these are grounds for folding these hands.

ENTER STRONG EARLY, WEAK LATE

The earlier your position, the stronger your cards need to be to enter the pot. The later your position, the weaker your cards can be.

If you have aces and kings and a player comes in raising before you, reraise. But if you have a non-premium hand, fold. Lean towards just calling with A-K and Q-Q. If the raiser is tight, fold with A-Q and J-J, but if the raiser is loose, raising or calling are both viable options. Remember, no play is set in stone in no-limit hold'em. Judge hands on a situation-by-situation basis.

Pass on all other hands from early position, especially against an aggressive table. If the table is tight or if it's early in a tournament and it just cost a lot to enter the pot, you can take a flier on a hand now and then to mix it up.

EARLY POSITION STARTING CARDS

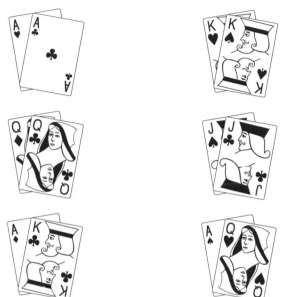

Middle Position

In middle position, you can play more hands simply because you have fewer players behind you who can raise your bets. If someone raises before it's your turn to act, consider folding all non-premium hands. You don't want to go into the flop as a big underdog, which your opponent's raise probably indicates since he's in an earlier position. And if the raiser is a tight player, fold J-J and A-Q as well. If you have A-A or K-K, reraise and have no fear of getting all your chips in the middle. You can also reraise with Q-Q and A-K, or you could just call.

If no one has raised in front of you, you will still play the premium hands for a raise and can add the second tier hands—8-8, 9-9, 10-10, as well as A-J, A-10, and K-Q—to your list of raising hands.

What happens if a player behind you reraises? If a player sitting behind you reraises, consider throwing second tier

CARDOZA PUBLISHING   AVERY CARDOZA

hands away. These hands have value, but against heavy betting, they're chip burners. Of course, if your opponent is low on chips and moves in on the preflop, especially in a tournament, give him credit for holding lesser quality cards and be prepared to play all premium hands—but again, use judgment. When in doubt, go with your gut feeling.

First, you have to look at who's raising. If you believe the player is on a bluff, consider calling. Further, if he's short-stacked and appears to be making a desperate play, you might play with him. Another time to consider calling is when you think your opponent has read you for a steal and is on a resteal. You might also believe that the player thinks you're weak and is trying to bully you. However, the majority of times, you have to give the raiser credit for holding strength. He is telling you that he has a better hand than yours, and you probably want to respect that and give up the pot. Weaker hands cannot stand a lot of heat.

You can also consider **limping** (calling and not raising) into the pot with the A-J, A-10, and the middle pairs. However, as a general rule, push at the pot and keep pressure on your opponents. Raising gives you the opportunity to win the pot right there while calling means that you must continue fighting for it on the flop. If your raise is called, you'll know that your opponents fear the strength you've shown. You'll have more leverage after the flop with a good chance to get a free card, or make a stab at the pot if your opponents checks to you. And you'll have lots to think about if someone bets into you.

60   WSOP: TOURNAMENT NO-LIMIT HOLD'EM

MIDDLE POSITION STARTING CARDS

Late Position

You can play many more hands in late position than in early or middle position simply because few players are sitting behind who can raise your bets or reraise your raises and force you to fold. For example, if you are the player sitting one seat in front of the button (the **cutoff seat**), only the button and the two blinds can raise; and if you are on the button, you only have to worry about the two blinds. If the blinds play with you, they have the decided disadvantage of having to act before you on every round thereafter—that's three more betting rounds—the flop, turn and river. That's a huge disadvantage to them. So when you're sitting on the button or in the cutoff seat, you have many more hands that you can play safely and profitably.

This allows you to play hands you would not think about playing in middle position, and certainly not in early position. If there have been raises prior to the action coming around to you, you can simply fold marginal hands without any cost at all, saving bets and chips. And that is why position is so important in hold'em.

If no one has raised the pot, you can expand your starting hands to any pair, an ace with any other card, and any two cards 10 or higher, Q-10 or K-J for example. Generally, it's best to come in raising. Most of the time, you'll win the blinds, which is good. If you get callers, your hand has enough value to see the flop.

If you're in late position in an unraised pot, all pairs are playable. In addition to the premium pairs (jacks through aces) and the middle pairs (eights through tens), you can now play 2-2 through 7-7. If you can see the flop cheaply, you can also play suited connectors that are 5 or higher, such as 5-6, 6-7, 7-8, 8-9, and 10-J. You are hoping to make two pair, trips, straight or flush draws with these types of hands—or best of all, a made straight or flush.

If you are dealt A-A or K-K in late position, raise if you think somebody will call your raise. If not, it might be better to limp in. You don't get kings or aces often, but when you do, you want to make money with them.

Late positions are steal positions. When you're playing in a steal position, your opponents will not give you as much credit for a good hand because they're figuring you to steal the pot. Of course, sometimes you will be doing exactly that. You should give them less credit for strong hands as well. So when you catch good on the preflop, you are in great position to not only steal the blinds, but trap opponents who try to resteal against you, or who give you action because they think you're just playing your superior position.

If the situation is right for a steal—that is, you have players behind you who won't usually defend their blinds—any two cards are valid raising hands. You can steal with hands such as J-8, 9-7, 3-2— and even 7-2, the worst starting hand in hold'em.

PLAYING PREMIUM HANDS IN LATE POSITION

If you're in late position and a player in early position has raised the pot, reraise with A-A, K-K, Q-Q and A-K. If you get reraised, you may consider just calling with Q-Q and A-K. And if the raiser is tight and goes all-in, you probably want to release those hands. You certainly do not want to be in that reraised pot with J-J, A-Q, or anything less. But with aces and kings, you're always ready to play for all the marbles preflop.

If a player in middle position raises the pot, reraise with the top four hands, A-A, K-K, Q-Q, and A-K. How you play J-J and A-Q is a judgment call, but it may be safer just to call and see the flop.

LATE POSITION STARTING CARDS

 to

 to

(Suited Connectors)

Playing the Blinds

When you are sitting in either of the blinds, you have the advantage of going last in the first round of play, but the big disadvantage of going first in all other rounds. Sometimes you get lucky as the big blind and get either a free ride because no player has raised, or win a free pot because all players have folded.

Playing the blinds is easy. If you're in the small blind and everyone folds to you, or if there are only callers and you can see the flop cheaply, it's not a bad play to call the big blind. You may flop something pretty or if everyone checks to the showdown, you might win with better garbage than your opponent. If the cost is cheap to see three more cards, the profit potential is enormous if you catch a big hidden hand and get played with by an opponent. So, throwing away a few chips here and there is not costly when you consider the big windfall you may inherit if you flop a monster.

If there is no raise and you're in the big blind with a hand you don't want to raise with, always see the flop for free. Don't make the mistake of folding!

If anyone raises from early or middle position, fold anything except premium hands. You're asking for trouble when you bump up against players showing strength, especially when you'll have to act before them on the next three betting rounds. If there is a raise from late position, suspect the player for a steal, especially if he has made a habit of raising from the cutoff or the button. You'll need to start defending your blinds if your opponents constantly try to steal them, so pick a good spot to raise right back when you think you can force your opponent out of the pot. You can raise, of course, with all premium hands, as well as hands that you normally wouldn't play from early position but which do have some strength—ace-anything, K-Q, K-J, or any two high cards.

You are out of position in the blinds—that is, you're in an early betting position—so you will have to play first on every other betting round if you decide to enter the pot. You're vulnerable to raises behind you, so you need strength to play from the blinds. Keep in mind that you're in early position, so play your hands according to the advice in the early position strategy section.

Other Starting Hands: All Positions

PLAYING ACE-ANYTHING

Many new players get overly excited about hands containing an ace, particularly suited aces that have flush possibilities. However, ace-anything hands smaller than A-K can spell a lot of trouble for you.

With A-K, you hope to flop an ace or a king, either of which will give you top pair, top kicker. Unless your opponent has flopped a monster, you most likely have the best hand and can play it aggressively. For example, if two suited cards come on board, you'll want to put a big bet into the pot to protect your top pair-top kicker hand and chase opponents out of the pot. Your big bet takes away the correct odds for a player going for a flush or straight. Making top pair-top kicker on the flop means that you hit the flop—that is the value of A-K hands when they connect.

Problematic hands occur when you have less than a king as a kicker and an ace comes on the flop. Or if you start with two high cards and connect with one of them, but you don't have top pair-top kicker. These types of hands are called **trouble hands**, because when a trouble hand actually connects with the flop, the chances are good that it is outkicked or outpaired and subject to losing lots of chips. So, hands such as A-Q, A-J, K-Q—really ace-anything or king-anything—have to be played carefully if your opponents bet aggressively.

PLAYING TRASH

One great way to mix up your play and be unpredictable is to come into the pot raising with trash hands—starting cards that normally wouldn't be strong enough to play. You have three goals when you play with garbage:

1. Steal the blinds and antes.
2. Break an opponent if someone calls and you get a lucky flop. For example, if you enter the pot with 8-5 and the flop comes 4-6-7 or A-8-5, you've got a hand that is impossible for your opponent to put you on. And if his starting cards were A-K on the A-8-5 flop, he's way behind and stands to lose a bunch of chips.
3. If you come at the flop aggressively, you may be able to push your opponent off the pot with your double bluff regardless of what falls.

However, keep in mind that trash hands are just that—trash. In the long run, they're big underdogs to win if the betting goes to a showdown, so don't make a habit of playing garbage. But now and then just to mix things up, playing trash against the right opponents in the right situations can pay dividends.

DON'T USE TELEVISED POKER AS YOUR TEACHER

Many new players, excited by the world-class poker players they see on television, emulate the hands they see the pros playing at the final table. You may wonder why I don't advocate playing those hands. The answer is simple: Final table television poker is not a realistic reflection of how no-limit hold'em is played. So, if you follow what you learn by watching television, you're going to get destroyed at the game. There are four major reasons for this:

1. Very few hands are shown on television. This leads viewers to believe that the cards shown are the ones typically played in a regular game. The fact is, they are not. TV broadcasts don't show the many, many hands that players have tossed away.

2. You're not getting a sense of tournament dynamics, where a player is often forced to make moves to protect a short stack, while another bets on cards to mix up his game. Other times, he may spot an opportunity that is not about the cards, but the situation.

3. You're often watching short-handed tables or heads-up action, where the hands that are correct to play are entirely different from tables with a full complement of eight or more players.

4. A trash hand may be featured because the play of it was interesting or the pot was large. For every hand shown, there may be hundreds that were played and not shown. The hands actually televised usually are not at all representative of the typical ones played.

For many players, the most confusing aspect of playing no-limit hold'em is deciding how many chips to bet. The next chapter gives you the scoop on how to bet the correct amount.

BETTING THE RIGHT AMOUNT

You find a hand you want to play, but now you wonder how much to bet. You look down at your stack. You can choose to risk anything from the minimum bet to all your chips.

What to do?

Making a bet for the right amount is surprisingly easy— if you know what you're trying to accomplish. Let's lay the groundwork right now.

WHAT BETTING IS ALL ABOUT

In poker, you're always competing for the pot—you want to win as much as you can on every hand you play. You make bets for one of three reasons:

1. You believe that your hand has enough strength to win and you want to induce opponents to put more money into the pot.
2. You want to force opponents out of the pot so that the field is narrowed, since having fewer players to compete against increases your chances of winning.
3. You want to induce all your opponents to fold so that you can win the pot uncontested.

Some players base the size of their bets on the strength of their hand. Mistake. Once opponents figure that out—and soon they will—it will be very easy for them to play against you and either blow you out of a pot when you have the better hand, or draw you deeper into a pot when they have the better hand.

Profitable poker is about deception. To achieve this goal in no-limit hold'em, you don't want to give your opponents any extra information. That means never showing them your cards unless they pay to see them at the showdown, and never tipping them off by making bets that reflect the strength of your hand. You achieve this deception by always betting or raising the same amount for the same type of situation. That way, when you bet, opponents are not wondering how strong your hand is, but whether you *have* a hand.

Big difference!

By being deceptive, you keep them off-balance, and that's exactly where you want them.

BETTING BEFORE THE FLOP

If no player before you has entered the pot on the first round of betting, you have three choices:

* Fold your hand
* Raise the Blind
* Call the Blind

1. Folding

When your hand is not going to be profitable, it's best to fold. Calling with a weak hand has its virtues as discussed earlier, but can lead to losses if an aggressive or tight player takes the pot away from you on the preflop or flop. If this happens to you enough times, you begin to realize that the better play would have been to fold in the first place. If you clearly understand that before you donate chips to an opponent, you will be that many chips richer.

2. Raising

Raising makes opponents pay to play. And it allows you to take the lead in betting. Both results are good things. Raising allows you to limit the field or eliminate it altogether, giving you the pot. If an opponent sees the flop with you, another bet will often eliminate him, or make him start playing scared— unless he hits the flop big.

If you're the first player coming into the pot on the preflop, you generally want to enter the pot with a **standard raise**, about three times the size of the big blind. If the big blind is at 50, make your raise 150; and if it's 100, make your raise 300. The reason you don't raise two times the big blind is that you make it too easy for your opponents, particularly the big blind, to enter the pot cheaply with marginal cards. When you let your opponents in cheap, you are subjecting your hand to lucky draws from players who might not otherwise have seen the flop.

A raise three times the size of the big blind is large enough to make it unprofitable for opponents to play marginal cards and trash. In other words, it takes away their favorable odds of seeing the flop (and possibly drawing good)—something that would not be achieved with a raise two-times the size of the big blind (as in limit hold'em).

So, when no players have entered the pot, you want your preflop raises to consistently be about three times the size of the big blind so that opponents get no extra information on the strength of your hand. Players that vary their preflop raises are sometimes announcing the strength of their hands.

And if one, two or three of your opponents have limped in to see the flop before it's your turn, make it four times the big blind if you have a raising hand. With more money in the pot, you want to make it unprofitable for the limpers to call your raise and continue playing. Plus, you would like to collect all their bets on the spot.

HOW MUCH TO RAISE PREFLOP
• When you are the first player to enter the pot, raise three times the size of the big blind.
• If one, two or three players limp into the pot, raise four times the size of the big blind.

3. Calling

Of the three options, calling is often the worst choice of all. Here's why:

A. If you come in weak (call) with *marginal* cards, a player after your position can raise and force you out.

Result: You've donated chips.

For example, you call with K-J from middle position, there are two callers and then a substantial raise before it gets back to you. You're best off folding before tossing away any more chips.

B. If you come in weak (call) with *premium* cards, you allow opponents with marginal hands to see the flop with hands that might connect and improve to beat you.

Result: You've allowed them to take your pot away, possibly at a big cost, because you'll be defending those chips while you're second best. For example, let's say you call with A-A or K-K and see the flop four-handed. You now have three opponents who can connect with the three cards in the middle. What happens if you bet the pot and are greeted by a huge raise? Maybe you have the best hand, maybe not. It may be a difficult call for you to make. Or what happens if you just call and give opponents a free card? Now you're either really asking for trouble or getting no value out of a rare premium pair.

There is a place for calling. When you want to see the flop cheaply with marginal cards, hoping to sneak in there and connect for a big hand, or when you want to slowplay pocket aces or kings for a big trap hand, calling can be an effective play. But generally speaking, for most players, calling is the worst option of your three choices.

Now, let's see what the dealer lays out in the middle of the table on the flop. Those first three community cards will be the signal for us to stop and fold, or go ahead and play.

WINNING STRATEGY ON THE FLOP: STOP OR GO?

You're in to see the flop with one or more opponents. You watch the dealer turn over the three community cards. Now you have to make some decisions. It's your turn to play. What to do?

BETTING ON THE FLOP

You have three choices on the flop:

- Fold
- Bet
- Check

Much of what was covered in the preflop section also applies on the flop. Taking the lead and pushing players gives you a better chance of winning the pot than playing passively. If you bet, your opponents may fold, and you will win. If you don't bet, they won't fold—but you might fold if one of them takes the lead instead.

When you are the first to bet after the flop, a pot-sized bet is standard. So if 350 is in the pot, bet around 350. If you're in a tournament with a pot sitting at 3,000, push 3,000 out there. Pot-sized bets make it expensive for marginal hands to call and give hands of decent strength reason enough to reconsider the price of entry.

You can sometimes get the same results by **underbetting** the pot—making a bet that is one-third smaller than the size of the pot or less—but the best play is usually to go with pot-sized bets.

Overbetting the pot means making a bet that is greater than about one and one-half the size of the pot. For example, betting around 1,500 when the pot has about 1,000 in it. You can also overbet the pot by going all in, which really puts opponents to the test. When you overbet, you're looking to get opponents to fold, or sometimes to trap them into calling when you have a great hand and they suspect you for a bluff.

HOW MUCH SHOULD YOU BET ON THE FLOP?

- When you are the first player to enter the pot, raise about the size of the pot.
- Underbetting the flop or overbetting the flop are plays that also can be effective.

THINKING ON THE FLOP

When the flop hits the board, the real play in hold'em begins. Unless you have the **nuts**, the absolute best hand possible given the cards on board, nothing is for sure when the flop hits the table. You might get a great flop, but an opponent might have flopped something even better. Most of the time, however, you will flop nothing—and your opponents will be in the same predicament.

So who gets the pot when neither player makes a powerful hand?

In no-limit hold'em, it is the player who goes out and gets it. Betting, raising, and putting pressure on the game causes opponents to fold. Great players keep pushing their opponents with bets and raises and take the pot right there or on the next betting round with continued aggressive play. If that doesn't work, they're able to read their opponents for strong hands and fold before they lose too many chips and get hurt.

So we're back to the two themes of what makes a successful poker player: *aggression* and *reading opponents*.

If you came in raising preflop, you want to continue playing aggressively. If you're first, bet regardless of what flops. Your opponent will probably fold and you will win the pot. If he calls and you don't improve, you might consider checking on the turn. If he raises your bet, you'll have a tough call to make, but you'll need to consider giving up the hand unless you think you have better cards that he has. Now, if you're second and he checks to you, bet out at him.

What if he bets into you? If you miss the flop, give him the pot. Since you've shown strength preflop, his bet on the flop means that you're probably second-best.

When you have what you think is the best hand, your goal is to take the pot immediately, particularly when there are straight and flush draws possible (for example, two cards of the same suit or cards in sequence are on the board). You don't want opponents to play for another card cheaply, successfully complete their draws, and then destroy you with a hand that shouldn't even have seen another card. If opponents are going to beat you, make them pay to do it!

However, if you have an absolute monster like a full house or quads, you want to keep players in and extract more bets out of them. That often means checking and hoping that a free card will give them enough of a hand to continue.

It's not always easy to tell where you stand when the flop hits. You could be better, worse, or about even with your opponents. Poker players get their clues from how their opponents bet and react to bets and, with experience, you'll get better and better at it.

Let's look at a few situations to see how this might work.

Situation One

Let's say that you start out with 7-7 and the flop comes 7-J-Q, all in spades. This is a great flop for you—you've made a set! But you do have one big problem: Those three spades make a flush possible. You bet, an opponent raises to 500, you reraise to 1,500, and he pushes all his chips in the middle! Now what do you do? You've got a big decision to make. You have a powerful hand, a set of sevens, but if it's not the best hand, you lose all your chips—on one hand!

Situation Two

Or maybe you start out with big slick, A-K, and *almost* get a great flop: A-J-10 of mixed suits. You've got top pair, top kicker—aces with a king kicker. Normally you're feeling pretty good in this situation, except that your raise is met with an all-in reraise. If your opponent is holding K-Q, he's flopped a straight, and given his strong betting, you have to suspect that possibility. Of course, he could have J-10 for two pair, or A-J for a stronger two pair. Perhaps he has that same A-K. Players tend to play big cards in hold'em and all these scenarios are possible given his aggressive stance. He might even have pocket tens or jacks and be holding a set.

Maybe he's bluffing. And maybe he's not.

So what do you do? It depends, it *always* depends. *What does he have?* Well, that's going to cost all your chips to find out.

Now you're playing poker. If your opponent is tight, you have to give serious consideration to giving up this pot, and if he is a maniac, betting and raising wildly, you have to consider the opposite. On the surface, given the strong betting on this ace-high flop with all the possibilities we just discussed, he has to figure you for at *least* aces, so when he's coming back with an all-in raise, you have to figure him for something stronger. Folding your hand may be the best play, but you still have to evaluate the situation correctly to make the best decision.

Few situations come up in no-limit where the answer is always the same no matter what is going on. The key to making the best decision is understanding how your opponent plays and what he might have. "But," you might ask, "how can I guess what he has if I can't see his cards?"

My best answer is that, even though you cannot physically see his cards, you *can* see how he is betting. You can note how he reacts to the betting of opponents, and from what position at the table he makes his plays. You also have to consider what you believe he thinks about your play.

Sometimes you can get clues from how he reacts to situations physically. It's like a detective solving a case. He's working with incomplete information because he didn't witness the crime, just like you have incomplete information because you can't see your opponent's cards. The detective can examine all sorts of information, sifting through the facts, weighing evidence and motives, until he has a pretty good clue as to what happened.

In poker, you're faced with a similar situation. You're given a bunch of clues, now you have to piece them together. By paying close attention to how an opponent plays, you can sometimes get a pretty good idea of where you stand in a hand.

You'll be wrong on occasion. Sometimes you will be bluffed out of pots where you have the best hand and sometimes you'll get suckered into pots where your opponents have the best hand. But again, that's poker. You won't always be right. However, the more you study the game and the more you play, the more accurate you will get at reading opponents and situations.

FIFTEEN IMPORTANT THINGS TO THINK ABOUT ON THE FLOP

1. If you miss the flop and an opponent bets into you, strongly consider folding. For example, if you start with A-K and the flop comes J-8-7, you've got nothing. Maybe your opponent is bluffing, but so what? You can't win every hand. And maybe he's not bluffing. Either way, you don't have much.

2. Suppose you start with a medium or small pocket pair and don't catch a third card to form a three of a kind. Bet if you think you can take the pot and check if you don't think you can. In other words: no set, no bet. You've missed the flop. Be careful about investing more chips into it.

3. If you start with a medium or small pocket pair and *catch* a third card to form a set, you're sitting pretty and want to extract as many chips as possible out of your opponents. That might mean either betting because they expect you to bet, checking to let them catch up with another card on the turn, or letting them take the lead if they're aggressive.

4. Trouble hands part A: Hands like A-Q, A-J, and A-10 are called trouble hands because if an ace flops, they're vulnerable to aces with bigger kickers. If you see a flop such as A-J-5 when you have A-Q and your opponent holds A-K, you can get hurt pretty badly. You would rather see the queen, your kicker, connecting. A flop of Q-10-3 is much better for the A-Q because you now have top pair and top kicker.

5. Trouble hands part B: Hands like K-Q and K-J are called trouble hands because if a king flops, your hand is vulnerable to the A-K. In a raised pot, be

careful because that raise indicates preflop strength, which may be trouble for you.

6. Pocket kings are the second-best hand you can start with, but if an ace flops, you can get into deep trouble if an opponent holds a pocket ace. In 2005, a player at my table busted out of the Main Event of the World Series of Poker after less than 45 minutes of play because he played K-K for an all-in bet *after* an ace flopped. He was shocked when he lost the hand and all his chips—but nobody else at the table was surprised.

7. Similarly, pocket queens lose their luster if an ace or king flops, especially given that players are more likely to play high cards. Pocket queens want to see flops such as J-8-6, where there are no overcards to the queen.

8. If you're drawing to a straight, you have to be concerned about two suited cards on the flop and *very* concerned if there are three suited cards on the board. Always be aware of flush possibilities when you're drawing to a straight.

9. If you start with a big pocket pair, you're probably still ahead on the flop as long as there are no overcards, no pair on board (possible three of a kind, full house, or quads), and no straight or flush draws. Make opponents put chips into the middle if they want to play with you.

10. Suppose you flop a set but are worried that an opponent has flopped a bigger set. For example, you start out with 4-4 and the flop is J-7-4. The simple strategy here is to play your set of fours like it is the boss. Set over set is possible, yes, but you can't play scared. The same goes before the flop when you get into a betting war holding kings and

are worried about your opponent having pocket rockets. As poker players say, "You can't get away from that hand."

11. When you've got the lead and the flop comes with cards that give opponents straight or flush draws, bet heavy and make them pay the price to go for their draws. For example, if you have A♦ K♥ and the flop is K♠ 10♠ 6♥, you've made top pair top kicker, but one more spade gives an opponent a possible flush. Make a pot-sized bet so that it will be unprofitable for an opponent to call. If you don't take the pot there, you'll be letting him play cheaply. If another spade falls and an opponent bets big, he either takes you out of the pot (maybe even on a bluff) or you'll play with him. Win or lose, you shouldn't have allowed him to play.

12. You flop top pair-top kicker. For example, suppose you have A-K and see the flop come with A-10-3 or K-J-4. Bet and make opponents pay to play, you're probably leading. If they fold, take the pot—it's yours. However, be careful if an opponent plays back at you for a lot of chips. Suspect a big hand or big draw.

13. You have an overpair to the flop. Let's say that you start with pocket nines and the flop comes 8-5-2. Bet and make opponents pay to see more cards or allow them to give you the chips in the middle.

14. You have an underpair to the flop; say a pair of fours. The flop comes J-8-6. You don't necessarily have the worst hand against an opponent who is playing aggressive and pushing you around. It's a tough call to make if he bets into you, but sometimes your instincts will tell you to play against some bets. If you read your opponent for a hand such as an A-K

or A-Q, you've got the better hand. These kinds of situations occur all the time in no-limit hold'em.

15. You don't always have to bet the flop. Change up your play sometimes. Don't be predictable. Giving a free card is not always a bad thing. It depends. *It always depends.*

Now it's time to see one more community card. The turn card can make or break your hand. In the next chapter, we'll detail important strategies for playing after you've seen six of the seven cards that will form the final destiny of your hand.

WINNING STRATEGY ON THE TURN: MAKE OR BREAK?

You're really into the hand now. You've played your starting cards preflop through the flop, and now you watch as a fourth card hits the board. It's your turn to play. What to do?

BETTING ON THE TURN

You have five options on the turn:

- Fold
- Check
- Underbet the pot
- Make a pot-sized bet
- Overbet the pot

You have to ask yourself whether you want your opponent to put more chips into the pot or fold and give the pot to you? You encourage him to fold, of course, by putting chips into the pot (betting). **Underbetting**, that is, making a bet that is smaller than one-third the size of the pot—encourages an opponent to play with you and get his chips in the middle. You're making it cheap for him. Making a **pot-sized bet**—one that is about the full size of the pot—usually induces an opponent to fold because of the cost. By putting even more chips into the pot than that, you'll give him extra encouragement.

The more chips you bet, the more reason an opponent has to fold, but at the same time, the more risk you take if he doesn't fold and has the better hand. If you overbet the pot as a way to get an opponent to fold, you risk more chips than you need to get the job done. Overbetting is generally not the best idea on the turn.

If you think a particular bet will get an opponent to lay down stronger cards, make that bet. If you think you have the best hand, try to get more chips into the pot. You don't want to give opponents a chance to improve their hands for free.

HOW MUCH SHOULD YOU BET ON THE TURN?

If you have the best hand and believe that you can get the better hand to lay down his cards—or if you want to build the pot—the most effective bets on the turn are usually at least one-third less than the size of the pot up to the full size of the pot, depending on the situation.

THINKING ON THE TURN

The turn is a betting round that will test your people-reading skills. How will your opponents react to a bet or check if you go first, and how will you react if they go first?

If you've played aggressively on the preflop and flop and your opponent hasn't budged, you have to figure him for possible strength. It's time for you to look at what you think *he thinks* you have. If you're representing strength and playing tight, you have to give him credit for a strong hand and slow down your betting unless you're confident that you've got a better hand. If he checks, you check, and if you're first, check to him and see how he reacts.

The turn is a time to put the brakes on a bluff that didn't work, and thus possibly ease your way into the river with a hand that can't weather much more betting. If your opponent is weak, he may check along with you. His check may be a clue: Perhaps you can zap him out on the river or play it slow and see who shows down the better hand. You can always push your bluff one more bet, but since your opponent saw you through on the flop, your bluff could put you in danger.

You felt out your opponents on the flop. How they played on the flop greatly influences the types of hands you think they may be playing. Use your best judgment and go with it. If you think a bet may push a weak opponent out of the pot, betting is a strong option. If you're not sure, checking is not a bad option. And if you think you have the best hand, try your best to get more chips into the pot. Of course, if he bets and you're weak, the best play may be to fold and give up the pot.

Situation

Suppose you came into the pot from late position with two connecting cards such as J♦ 10♣. The flop came K♣ Q♦ 6♠ and you called a single raise with two other opponents in the pot. You're three-handed on the turn. Now the board is K♣ Q♦ 6♠ 4♠, so you still have a draw to what you figure is the best hand, but if you don't catch, you've got nothing. The turn brought a second spade on board, giving any opponent with two spades in the hole a possible draw to a spade flush, but you're less concerned with the possibility of a flush than if the *flop* had those two spades which, like you, would have given him incentive for a draw—but a better one than your straight. In that case, you wouldn't want to weather too much betting and, of course, you'd have to completely shut down if another spade came down. But still, with two suited on board, you have to keep the backdoor flush in mind as a possibility.

You'd like to have both of your opponents check to you here so you can get a free card, but no such luck. Your first opponent bets the size of the pot from an early position. Opponent two calls the raise. You're at the World Series of Poker and this hand is shaping up to have a bunch of chips in it. What do you do?

In a tournament, your first consideration is the chips. How many you have, how many your opponents have, and how many are in the pot are the very first things you need to consider. As I will stress elsewhere in this book, in a tournament, it's all about the chip counts. Your decision here, as in every other situation, will be influenced by them.

Okay, so how many chips do you have?

Let's say you have 7,500 worth of chips in front of you. By itself, that says nothing, because chips are always relative. If the blinds are 25/50, you're fairly deep-stacked and can afford a small call for a chance to win a decent-sized pot. If the blinds, on the other hand, are 1,500/3,000, you're severely short-stacked and have no business being in this pot in the first place, not with your tournament on the line.

But what if the blinds are 200/400 and the cost to enter the pot is 1,500 to see the river? This is a large amount relative to your stack size, all on a draw you probably won't get. And if you do get the draw, what if that 9 is a spade, you bet, and your tight opponent goes all in?

In this situation, with a draw on the turn and 20 percent of my chips to see the river, I'd probably let the hand go.

Another possibility is to go all in, hoping to win the pot by default if both opponents fold. The problem here, though, is that you've got *two* opponents to contend with, greatly increasing the chances that one will call your bluff. Do they view you as a bluffer, or as a tight player? Do they have so many chips committed to the pot that they will feel obligated to call or do they have such a big stack that calling is no big deal if one of them suspects you for a bluff. You have to consider these factors, because if you're wrong and you lose, your tournament is finished. It will be the last piece of speculation you'll do in this WSOP event. Of course, you also have the chance that you will get called and hit your straight, making you feel brilliant (or lucky).

Personally, unless I was very confident that my opponents were going to fold, I wouldn't attempt a bluff here. I'm not fond of calling on a coin flip for my tournament life; to go in as a 1 in 5 dog would be foolish.

And if I had lots of chips? I might make the call if there were enough chips in the pot to justify the call (pot odds) or my opponents had lots of chips also, giving me the chance to get them for a very big pot if I make the straight and they play with me (implied odds). If they had few chips and there wasn't much to get from them, or much in the pot, I might give up the pot right there and save my chips for a better situation.

We started this discussion on the turn, but really we would have to backtrack before the flop and see what you were doing in this pot in the first place—maybe you got in cheaply or tried to steal the blinds and picked up a few callers—and then pick up the thinking from there. Without going into the entire hand, my point is that every play you make, be it a bet, raise, fold or check, is interrelated with the earlier streets in the hand, the player and table dynamics, and of course, the relative chip counts and blinds. In other words, no play can be made in a vacuum of knowledge. But where we stood on the turn in this instance, given the little knowledge presented, I'd be inclined to preserve my chips if they were scarce.

WINNING STRATEGY ON THE RIVER: SINK OR SWIM?

The last card hits the board. You're looking at the five cards that you share with your opponents to make your final hand. The pot is either going to be yours or it will belong to an opponent. It may depend on how the betting goes.

BETTING ON THE RIVER

You have six options, depending on your position:

- Check
- Check-raise
- Underbet the pot
- Make a pot-sized bet
- Go all in
- Fold

When you have a big hand that you're confident is the best, you want to get more chips into the pot. Sometimes this means underbetting the pot, sometimes it means making a pot-sized bet, and sometimes it means going all-in.

You have to know your opponents to make the best play. If you're last to bet and no one has bet in front of you, put the amount of chips in the pot that you think your opponents will call. If you're first, you have two options: check or bet. If your opponent is very aggressive or has been leading at the pot, you can consider checking and letting him bet, then going over the top of him with a raise to try and get more chips in the pot.

You want to be careful not to move an opponent holding a losing hand off a pot with a bet, but at the same time, you want to get more chips into the middle. Checking risks "losing" chips you could have sucked into the middle with the proper size bet. Often, making an underbet is a good way to get more chips out of your opponent. You make it tempting enough so that he believes he has to call. Your knowledge of how your opponent plays should guide you. Every situation and every opponent calls for a different answer.

When you're bluffing, going with a pot-sized bet or an oversized or all-in bet can put enough chips on the table to force out an opponent. Beginners sometimes make the mistake of bluffing too timidly on the river, tossing in too few chips relative to the pot size. If you're going to bluff at the river, make sure it's for enough chips that your opponent will be faced with a difficult decision about whether to call.

The worst thing you can do on the river is attempt to bluff out a player who is either holding a monster hand, or is a calling station! We all have our stories of trying to bluff out nut flushes and full houses—somehow, they don't move off the pots so easily. It happens sometimes, but if you pay careful attention, you'll mostly avoid this unpleasant surprise.

And bluffing against a calling station? If he's called every bet to the river, do you really expect him not to call this time?

HOW MUCH SHOULD YOU BET ON THE RIVER?

- If you're not sure that you have the best hand, strongly consider checking. If you bet and an opponent's raise will drive you from the pot, making that first bet may be a mistake.
- If you do have the best hand, bet the amount that will get you a call.
- Bluffing with any size of bet—underbetting the pot or making an all-in bet—can be a big play here but proceed carefully. Don't take foolish risks.

THINKING ON THE RIVER

When you have a reasonable hand but have doubts about whether it's the best one out there, it's often better to check at the river, rather than bet. Here's why:

1. A player who is holding a better hand usually will call you. This loses both the pot *and* your river bet.
2. If an opponent raises you, you'll probably have to fold, again losing both the pot and your river bet.
3. If your opponent has a weak hand, he'll usually fold, so you get no extra chips.
4. If you bluff-bet against a loose player who always calls, you risk losing the whole pot.

In the first two situations, you've lost not just the pot, but your river bet as well. Minimizing lost chips is essential to winning at poker. In the third instance, you haven't lost chips, but you've risked chips to win a hand you would have won anyway.

If you check with a hand of moderate strength and your opponent checks, you'll see the showdown with no further cost. If he bets, you see what you want to do.

You should bet first on the river only when you feel reasonably confident that you can get an opponent with a better hand to fold, or when you want to get more chips into the pot because you feel you have a better hand.

If an opponent checks to you, and you have the best hand, bet so that you get value for the cards—but only if you're confident that your opponent doesn't have you pegged as an aggressive player that he can trap with a check-raise. Bluffing is always an option—but again, it must be for enough chips to be effective—as is checking to see the showdown.

Now it's time to turn to an integral part of any poker game, especially no-limit hold'em. How you adjust your play according to how many outs you have and how much money you can win if you make your hand is the subject of the next chapter.

 # HOW OUTS & ODDS INFLUENCE YOUR PLAY

Anytime you're contemplating risking money on a hand—that is, putting chips into the pot—the real question is, "Will it make me money?" If you can determine that the risk is worth the reward—that the bet will give you profits in the long run—then it is a good play. And if the play is not profitable in the long run, it isn't a good play.

Poker players use two tools to get a handle on this: pot odds and implied odds. First of all, don't get intimidated by the complicated-sounding terms, which, upon your initial glance, may make you want to stick your head under a pillow and groan. I'm going to make the concepts easy to digest. So take the pillow away. You already use some form of these concepts all the time though you might not realize it. When you choose to go to a movie, you do so because you believe it will be worth your time and money. When you buy a car, a house, or a collectible—really any purchase at all—you always ask yourself if the item is worth the cost.

It is the same in poker. If a play will make money in the long run, you make the play, and if not, you don't. While you never really know exactly where you stand on a hand when you're contesting a pot, or how much money might end up in the pot by the time all the betting is complete, you can make educated guesses. You determine if it is worth putting more money in the pot based on your perceived chances of winning

and the reward you would get if you prevail. In other words, is it a good bet?

Every time you're faced with a betting decision, try to get a sense of whether or not you've got the best hand. If you feel you don't, decide whether or not the money you'll have to invest in the pot is worth the amount of money you might win should your cards come home. Put simply: risk versus reward. In the long run, will you make money?

So how do you determine if a play is profitable? How do you know when the risk of putting more chips into the pot is worth the reward?

If you believe you have the best hand, it's a no-brainer—you always want more money in the pot. But if you think your hand needs to improve to win, you need to be aware of your chances of improving to a winner. All discussions of pot odds and implied odds start with a basic question: How many chances do you have to win? Poker players use a concept called "outs" to determine the answer to that question.

HOW DO YOU KNOW HOW MANY OUTS YOU HAVE?

Outs are the cards that will make your hand strong enough to win. For example, if you are all-in with two kings against an opponent with two aces and there is one card to come, you know you have two outs—the two remaining kings. No other card that comes on the river will improve your hand to a winner.

But unless you're all-in with your opponent, you'll never really know how many outs you have because you won't be able to see your opponent's cards. So calculating outs is not an exact science. But you do know your own cards and can easily determine your chances of improving to a stronger hand. And you can get a sense of where an opponent might be with his cards, based on how the betting is going and your knowledge of his play.

For example, say you have J♣ 10♣ and the board is A♣ 8♣ 6♥ 3♦.

YOU   YOUR OPPONENT

THE BOARD

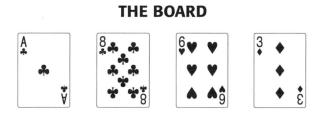

On the turn, your opponent bets into you. You figure him for aces, perhaps a high pocket pair, hands you'll easily beat if you get another club to fill your flush draw. However, if you don't improve, you appear to have almost no chance of winning. After all, what can your unpaired J-10 beat? Not much. And if you pair your jack or 10 on the river, you'd still be second best to all sorts of hands. You figure to need a club to win. There are nine clubs remaining in the deck, so you have nine outs.

If there was a 7♥ instead of a 6♥ on the board, you would have an additional three outs—9♦, 9♥, and 9♠—due to the inside straight draw possibility, for a total of 12 outs. (You wouldn't include the 9♣ because it is already being counted as one of your flush cards.)

THE REMAINING CLUBS
Your Nine Outs

WHAT ARE YOUR WINNING CHANCES?

You know six cards, your two pocket cards and the four on the board. Since the deck has 52 cards, that leaves 46 unknown cards. Nine of those cards—the nine remaining clubs of the original 13 in the deck (you have two of those clubs and the board has two)—will improve your flush draw to a winner. The remaining 37 cards will lose. So the math is simple: 37 ways to lose, 9 ways to win (37 to 9), or a little more than 4 to 1 against with just one card to come.

Obviously, you're more likely to lose with this hand than win, and based on that alone, you'd never make the call. But there is another factor to consider: how many chips can you win? There is a reason people play the lottery even though they have almost no chance of winning and why poker players make calls and bets, even though they're an underdog to win the pot. And that reason is the *payoff.*

So is it worth calling the bet to see more cards? To answer this question, we need to see if the payoff is good enough, and if it is, then it's worth calling the bet.

Now we turn to pot odds and implied odds to get our answer.

HOW DO YOU CALCULATE YOUR POT ODDS?

Pot odds is the amount of money in the pot *including* what your opponent has already bet—because that money is in the pot, and he can't take it back—against what it will cost you to call the bet. For example, if 50 is in the pot, and you need to call a bet of 10 to play, you are getting pot odds of 5 to 1. So, in this situation, you can win 50. The question is: are your winning chances better than 5 to 1, which would be giving you good pot odds and make this a good bet, or worse than 5 to 1, which would be giving you bad pot odds and make this a bad bet?

In the earlier example where we had J-10, we determined that we had about a 4 to 1 chance of getting a club on the river. So with a payoff of 5 to 1 in a situation where it is only 4 to 1 against making the club flush, it is a good bet to make.

Let's look at another situation. Suppose there's 300 in the pot and your opponent bets the size of the pot, another 300. Now there is 600 available to be won. It will cost you 300 to see the raise and have a chance to win that 600, so you are getting pot odds of 2 to 1. If you're on a flush draw or straight draw with one card to come and are figuring your hand to be about a 4 to 1 or 5 to 1 underdog, you are not getting enough of a return to make this a profitable call. On the other hand, if you figure your hand has about an even-money chance of winning, then you're getting great odds to make the call.

Here's another way to look at pot odds. Let's say that you are offered a proposition where you would bet $20 on a coin toss but could only win a total of only $1. You'd turn it down. You'd be getting the wrong odds—and how! The risk isn't worth the reward. However, if you would get $20 for every win, you'd have an even-money shot—a fair proposition.

But what if you could win $40 on that same flip of the coin? You'd be very happy to risk $20 to win $40. You have one chance in two of winning (1 to 1 odds)—the same as on the other two propositions—but you would be getting a 2 to 1 payoff! If you made this bet all day long, you would make a fortune, provided your host didn't wise up or run out of money.

You use pot odds to determine if going for the pot is justified by the amount you might win. If the bet will make you money in the long run, it's a good bet. Whenever you have a hand that is favored to win, the pot odds will always be favorable. But it is also correct to play hands even though you are *not* favored to win—provided there is enough of a payoff for the risk.

When you do play second-best hands, it should be because they give you good value, because your long term expectation is to win money in that particular situation. You may be an underdog in a hand, but if, in the long term, playing it gives you more profits than losses, you should play it. If the situation is ripe for a bluff and that might take down the pot, there is good value in betting or raising with a weaker hand. Your opponent may not fold, but if you estimate that he will fold enough times to make aggressive betting profitable in that type of situation, it's a good play. Playing only good hands will make you predictable and playing too many bad hands will bury you in losses. Profitable play requires you to strike a balance between the two extremes.

But there is one more element you need to consider. What if there is more betting to come in the hand, especially if you're playing no-limit and have a chance to get an opponent for lots of chips?

Aha! Now *there's* a key concept.

WHAT IS YOUR POTENTIAL GAIN, YOUR IMPLIED ODDS?

The amount *currently in the pot* (pot odds) is one thing, the amount that *might get into the pot* with further betting is another thing altogether. This concept is commonly called **implied odds**, though **potential gain** is an appropriate term as well, as the amount that might get into the pot is not implied but speculated.

By incorporating the concept of potential gain into your thinking, you increase the number of hands you might play in any form of poker but particularly in no-limit because of the large amount of chips that can be won in a pot. Whenever you play a hand, you must always consider the amount you stand to gain if you hit your cards and can induce an opponent to continue further into the hand—or he induces you, where, on that side of the coin, you need to figure out your risk! For example, in a tournament, if an opponent's stack is 5,000, you may consider that potential gain to be worth a certain amount of risk. On the other hand, if his stack is just 1,000, or if it is say 20,000, that may make a big difference in how you play your cards in a given situation.

So if a pot currently has 50 in it and you have a shot at getting 500 more by sneaking in there with a longshot hand and hitting it, it would be profitable to play more cards in the right circumstances. In other words, the cost is cheap and your hand would have a surprise value if it hit the board, giving you a chance to get lots of chips out of an opponent who couldn't

accurately guess the strength of your cards—in poker talk, he *couldn't put you on a hand.*

USE THIS SIMPLE RULE TO DETERMINE YOUR OUTS AND CHANCES OF WINNING

We've shown what happens on the turn with one card to come. What happens when you have that flush draw on the flop with two cards to come? Or if you have more or fewer outs? Where do you stand?

Luckily, there is a simple formula that will allow you to figure your winning chances when you know the number of outs. I call this **Cardoza's 4 & 2 Rule**. On the turn, where there is only one card to come, you multiply the number of outs by two for a reasonable estimate of your chances of winning. And on the flop, where you have *two* cards to come, you multiply the number of outs by four.

These calculations are not exact, nor do they need to be. You just need to know *approximately* where you stand. Since the concept of outs is an educated estimate and not a perfect calculation anyway (because you can never be completely sure of the strength of your opponent's cards), exact figures are irrelevant.

And for this purpose, multiplying by two or four shows you about where you're at.

CARDOZA'S 4 & 2 RULE ESTIMATING YOUR WINNING CHANCES	
Betting Round	**Multiply Outs by:**
The Flop	4
The Turn	2

If you have the same flush draw as in our earlier example, you have about a 20 percent chance of winning with one card to come, which we'll further simplify by rounding it up to a 20 percent chance of hitting your hand—again, a reasonable enough estimation to guide you along. If you had a flush draw on the flop, you'd multiply the 9 outs by 4, giving you about a 36 percent chance of winning, or roughly 1 chance in 3. Again, to make it simpler, we round it off to 35 percent. (Incidentally, the odds of making a flush are 35 percent and 19.6 percent, respectively, on the flop and turn, so you see we're pretty close using these estimates.)

Here is a chart that shows the number of outs you have for straight and flush draws.

CHANCES OF COMPLETION: STRAIGHT AND FLUSH DRAWS				
Hand	Example	Outs	FLOP Approx. Odds of Filling	TURN Approx. Odds of Filling
Straight Draw	5♣ 6♥ 7♠ 8♣	8 outs	2 to 1	5 to 1
Flush Draw	Q♦ 9♦ 7♦ 3♦	9 outs	2 to 1	4 to 1

SUMMING UP OUTS AND ODDS

Any time the betting action is up to you, make sure that the amount of money you invest will show a long term profit for you, meaning that the pot odds or the potential gain give you a healthy return on your investment of chips. If you quickly add up your outs, you'll have a sense of your winning chances.

Knowing your outs and your odds is extremely important to your success at poker, and particularly your success in no-limit hold'em tournaments.

Now that we know how to determine them, let's move right along by shuffling up and dealing ourselves into a World Series of Poker tournament. Part Three shows you how to win at the most exciting tournament game in the world.

Part 3

WINNING NO-LIMIT HOLD'EM TOURNAMENT STRATEGY

Winning a World Series of Poker tournament can be a life-changing experience. These prestigious events not only offer you a chance to compete for thousands of dollars in prize money in small-buy-in tournaments, but for tens of thousands, hundreds of thousands, and yes, millions of dollars in the large buy-in tournaments at the World Series of Poker.

And forgetting the money for a few seconds—and *only* for a few seconds—the competition and fun of tournament poker, especially no-limit hold'em, is simply lots of fun, worth every penny of your entry fee.

So what does it take to enter a poker tournament? Money. That's all. Unlike professional baseball, basketball, golf, or any other sport where you have to earn your way onto the professional circuit, the world of poker is purely egalitarian. Put up your money and you can play.

Whether played online or in a land-based casino, tournaments work pretty much according to the same principles. Even the biggest tournaments are open to all players who want to participate and are very simple to enter: just show up and hand over your entrance fee!

And how about the World Championship? Ditto. Put up the loot and put on your playing suit. You may be the lucky soul who goes all the way, as did Joe Cada, who won $8,547,042 in 2009 at the age of twenty-two.

Dream on, my friend, you could be next.

HOW
TOURNAMENTS
WORK

It's time to get your feet wet in the very exciting world of tournament poker. There's so much money to be made in the tournament games—and so much fun to be had—that it would be a shame for you not to play.

Of course, the big poker event that is at the epicenter of all poker players' dreams and aspirations is the World Series of Poker, held every summer in Las Vegas. The Main Event, the $10,000 buy-in no-limit hold'em championship, is the one that crowns the world champion. But the World Series is more than just the "big one." It is actually a series of over 50 events, each of which awards a gold bracelet, a championship title for the event, and bragging rights to the winner—plus a big first-place cash prize.

Most of the tournaments are no-limit hold'em events of various buy-ins ranging from $1,000 to $10,000, but there are also limit and pot-limit hold'em, seven-card stud, Omaha, some forms of draw poker (lowball, triple draw), and events that combine multiple games. In all, the championships span more than six weeks, with the Main Event taking more than ten days to conclude. The WSOP has also started a series of major tournaments held around the country in various locales, which are considered important events for the pros.

Are you a little nervous about what to do next? Not to worry. Just find a tournament anywhere that you want to play, pay your entry fee, and grab a seat. We'll go over all the basics in this chapter and then move on to specific winning strategies in the next few chapters.

REGISTER AS EARLY AS POSSIBLE

To get started in a tournament, you have to register and pay the entrance fee. The sign-up area is usually in the poker room. Otherwise, signs, the poker room employees, or fellow players will let you know where you can get registered. In the World Series of Poker, you will be required to show an I.D., so be sure to bring that along when you go to register.

The sign-up process is pretty easy. All you do is fill out a form and hand over the entrance fee. In return, you'll get a slip of paper assigning you to a table and seat where you will begin play at the allotted time. When you sit down to play, show the dealer your receipt. Unlike a cash game, you *cannot* change seats. The only possible exception is if two family members or husband and wife are at the same table, in which case it would be up to the tournament director to make changes.

In major tournaments at the World Series of Poker, the line forms several hours before the tournament is scheduled to begin. In order to avoid the hassles of a no-limit tournament that attracts thousands of players at the World Series, be sure to register well in advance. You can usually register up to a week or two before the event on the premises—and sometimes much earlier. You can also preregister for the WSOP by following the instructions on their website.

If you do come late, there is no penalty other than the chips you'll lose to the blinds once the tournament begins. This is not a huge loss as the blinds are small for the first few levels of play, but it is better to get acclimated as the tournament begins rather than come in late, feeling rushed and out of sync.

In smaller tournaments, you'll usually have no problem arriving at the last minute, as the fields are smaller and the tournament personnel have enough resources to get you signed up easily. But the no-limit events at the World Series of Poker, particularly the lower entry buy-ins of $1,000 that they run on Saturdays, are massive and might sell out. I recommend that you arrive at least 15 minutes before the scheduled start time if you've already bought your entry. Even better, give yourself 30 minutes. You'll have a good time chatting it up with the other players while you wait for the first cards to be dealt. Also, you want to get acclimated to the playing environment so that when the first cards are dealt, you've had a chance to shake out at least a few of the nervous jitters that go hand in hand with playing in a World Series of Poker event. I also like to have a time buffer so that outside events I cannot control, like traffic, or being confused about my seat assignment, don't interfere with getting to the tournament on time.

But to make sure you can get a place in the Saturday events, or other popular tournaments, you must register early, ideally, at least the day before the event. There are stories of players getting shut out of tournaments because they waited until the last minute and the tournament was sold out.

WHAT MAKES A TOURNAMENT EXCITING?

A **tournament** is a competition in which players start with an equal number of chips and play until one player holds all of them. It is a process of elimination, a gladiator contest where the last player remaining will be the winner. As players lose their chips and are eliminated from play, the remaining competitors get consolidated into fewer tables. What might start out as a 120-player event played at a dozen ten-handed tables will get reduced to eleven tables, and then ten tables, and so on, as players bust out.

Eventually, the field will be narrowed down to just one table, the **final table**, where the prestige and big money is earned. And that table will play down until just one player is left holding all the chips—the **champion**. Your goal is to be that last player so you can win the big prize, or at the very least, to finish **in the money**, that is, win a cash prize by finishing among the top players.

In big events, winners can take home in excess of one million dollars. The Main Event in the 2005 World Series of Poker awarded over $1 million dollars each to every one of the final table contestants! In fact the total prize pool of over $50 million in the final event alone made it the biggest money sporting event in the world! Not that, for example, the 2009 Main Event was too shabby either. Every final-table player again won at least $1 million, with the ninth-place finisher, James Akenhead, earning $1,263,602 and the main-event winner, Joe Cada, winning $8,546,435!

Every tournament player buys in for a set amount of money at the World Series of Poker. It could be any amount, $1,000 for the smaller buy-in events, or as much as $50,000 for the huge-buy-in tournament (the mixed games championship event)—depending upon the event you choose to play. In the WSOP circuit events, which are a series of more than 10 WSOP-branded events held around the country throughout the year, buy-ins can be as low as several hundred dollars.

Everyone loves the World Series of Poker tournaments because the prize pools are enormous, the action is as exciting as can be, and the winners will experience something they will talk about and remember for the rest of their lives.

FIVE WAYS TOURNAMENTS DIFFER FROM CASH GAMES

Tournaments and cash games differ from each other in five important ways:

1. **Starting chip counts.** In tournaments, all players start with the same number of chips. In cash games, players may start with as many chips as they want to buy within any minimum or maximum amounts that may be set by the cardroom.

2. **Getting more chips.** Unless the tournament is a rebuy or add-on event, once you lose your chips, you are eliminated. That's it—over and out! In rebuy and add-on events, players can only rebuy or add-on during the first three levels or so. After that, there is no coming back once you're eliminated. In cash games, you can always buy in for more chips.

3. **Cash value of chips.** Tournament chips are worthless at face value. They are only good within the tournament as a means of survival and power. Chips used in cash games are worth exactly the chip amount printed on the chip.

4. **Start and finish time.** Tournaments have a set starting time and end when you lose your chips, with the tournament itself ending when one player holds all the chips. In cash games, you can start and quit any time you want.

5. **Possible wins.** In bigger tournaments, the prize pools offer players a shot at huge lottery-sized winnings that, for the average player, would not normally be possible to win in a lifetime's worth of play. In cash games, the winning potential is mostly determined by the limits played.

TWO TYPES OF TOURNAMENTS: FREEZE-OUTS AND REBUYS

There are two types of tournaments—freeze-outs and rebuy tournaments. A **freeze-out tournament** is a do or die structure. Once you run out of chips, you are eliminated. Unlike a cash game, you can't go back into your pocket for more chips. All the tournaments at the World Series of Poker are freeze-outs.

In a **rebuy tournament**, you can purchase additional chips which is usually allowed only when your chip stack is equal to or less than the original starting amount and only during the first few specified rounds of play. This is called the **rebuy period**. Some tournaments allow limited rebuys, and others allow players to rebuy as often as they go broke, that is, until the rebuy period is over. At the end of the rebuy period, most tournaments allow you to get an **add-on** as well—a final purchase of a specific amount of additional chips. Once the rebuy period is over, you're playing in pure survival mode. If you lose your chips, you are eliminated and your tournament is over. The World Series of Poker used to offer rebuy tournaments, but discontinued them after 2008. You never know, though, they could be reinstated as part of the official program in coming years.

SATELLITES, MEGASATELLITES, SUPERSATELLITES

In the 1970s, the Horseshoe Casino in Las Vegas came up with a great concept to increase attendance in the Main Event of the World Series of Poker. It was pretty clear that few players could afford or were willing to cough up $10,000 entry fees. But if they could get in for less, they'd be there for sure.

And so they came up with a great concept: **satellites**. For a fraction of the cost of the Main Event, players could enter a one-table mini-tournament of ten players, where the winner would earn a seat into the Main Event. If a player put up $1,000 and beat the other nine players at his table, he'd have a $10,000 entry and a chance at the big prize. And that is exactly what happened to Tom McEvoy when he parlayed a satellite win into the World Championship in 1983 to become the first satellite winner ever to win the big one. In fact, Rod Peate, who placed second that year, also won his entry via a satellite.

Eventually, the satellite concept was expanded to include multiple-table tournaments that awarded entries to multiple winners. These events, called **megasatellites** or **supersatellites**, have become enormously popular. The supers and megas attract hundreds of players and can award dozens of seats to the top finishers in just one event. The World Series of Poker offers daily megasatellites twice nightly once the preliminary events begin, offering you many opportunities to win your way into the big one.

For the top finishers in these megas, it's a really inexpensive way to have a shot at millions. Other tournaments also may have relatively inexpensive super satellite entry fees for their main $10,000 or higher events, or they may make the entry fees $1,000. This allows many more players to win their entry, since one seat usually is awarded to every ten entrants.

It isn't only the World Series of Poker that offers satellites and megasatellites. Online poker rooms run tournament satellites as well and send thousands of satellite winners to the World Series of Poker every year. Interestingly, online sites often supply more players to the WSOP than any other source. That's how World Champion Chris Moneymaker got there in 2003. Moneymaker was able to parlay a $39 entry fee for an online tournament into a championship and $2.5 million. And in 2004, Greg Raymer turned an online entry into $5 million.

Second-place finisher David Williams, who also qualified online, earned $2.5 million. Not bad for a week's work.

If you want to try your hand at a major event, just keep your eyes open and you'll find plenty of opportunities to earn your way into it. To get an edge on your competition, you'll find strategies specifically designed for satellites later in this section of the book. But before we get to that, let's delve into how no-limit hold'em tournaments are structured. Read on.

THE STRUCTURE OF NO-LIMIT HOLD'EM TOURNAMENTS

Tournaments are divided into **levels**, also called **rounds**. Each level is marked by an increase in the amount of chips players are forced to commit to the pot before the cards are dealt. The blinds slowly increase, and after a few levels, the antes kick in. Levels may be as short as fifteen or twenty minutes in low buy-in events that are designed to be completed in as little as a few hours, or as long as ninety minutes to two hours for major events that are structured to last up to a week or more.

Each event is set up differently by the tournament director and the length of the rounds and structure for increasing the blinds and antes will be posted in advance on a board or printed on sheets that you can pick up in the playing area, usually near the registration desk.

In general, the greater the amount of money at stake, the longer the tournament. Short, quick rounds such as those used in low-limit events, make for faster play and introduce a greater element of luck as you're forced to play more aggressively to stay ahead of the quickly increasing blinds and antes. In the bigger events, you're given more chips to start, the levels are longer, and the increase in blinds and antes is more gradual so that you can get a lot more play. This combination lends itself to the skill factor playing a larger role in tournaments with longer and more gradual levels than is the case in the more hurried low-limit tournaments.

The typical World Series of Poker tournament has rounds that last one hour. In these tournaments, you will be given a 15 or 20 minute break after every two rounds, with a dinner break scheduled in after usually six rounds of play. If the event features 90 minute or two hour rounds, then the break will be after each round so that players get a chance to hit the bathrooms or catch a snack.

The speed of a tournament is regulated by the blind and ante structures. When the forced bets are low, there is no real pressure for players to play hands. You can sit and wait for premium hands and optimal situations. But as you advance deeper into a tournament, the blinds and antes become more expensive, and the price of sitting passively and not playing hands is high. If your stack isn't large enough, as few stacks are, you will get blinded and anted out if you don't make some plays.

Of course, in any tournament, no matter how big or how small—or any cash game as well—the element of luck is always a factor. However, the greater your level of skill and the better you play, the more chances you have of getting into the money or winning the tournament. Yes, there is luck, but never downplay the amount of skill involved in succeeding in tournament poker. Once you play your first event, this will be eminently clear. And the more you play, the more you'll see how your decision-making creates your own destiny and affects your chances of winning the whole pie.

Sometimes the turn of a card can make or break you in an event, but the events leading up to the decisive moment, the number of chips you gained or lost, and the decisions you made, all have a part.

Here is a fairly typical payout schedule. You'll notice that the first three rounds have only blind bets—it isn't until the fourth round that antes kick in as well.

$1,000 WSOP NO-LIMIT HOLD'EM STRUCTURE CHART

Following is the structure from the 2010 WSOP $1,000 Saturday no-limit hold'em tournaments. For the $1,000 buy-in, each player receives 3,000 in starting chips.

LEVEL	ANTE	BLINDS
1	-	25-25
2	-	25-50
3	-	50-100
4	-	75-150
5	-	100-200
6	25	100-200
7	25	150-300
8	50	200-400
9	75	300-600
Remove 25 Chips		
10	100	400-800
11	100	500-1,000
12	100	600-1,200
13	200	800-1,600
14	300	1,000-2,000
15	400	1,500-3,000
Remove 100 Chips		
16	500	2,000-4,000
17	500	3,000-6,000
Remove 500 Chips		
18	1,000	4,000-8,000
19	1,000	5,000-10,000
20	1,000	6,000-12,000
21	2,000	8,000-16,000
22	3,000	10,000-20,000
23	3,000	12,000-24,000
24	4,000	15,000-30,000
Remove 1,000 Chips		
25	5,000	20,000-40,000
26	5,000	25,000-50,000
27	5,000	30,000-60,000
28	10,000	40,000-80,000
29	10,000	50,000-100,000
30	15,000	60,000-120,000
31	20,000	80,000-160,000
32	30,000	100,000-200,000
33	30,000	120,000-240,000
34	40,000	150,000-300,000

WSOP TOURNAMENT DESCRIPTION

Players begin with 3,000 in Tournament Chips. All levels will last 60 minutes. Breaks will occur after every two levels and last 20 minutes. Dinner break on each Day 1 will be after the completion of level 6 and last 90 minutes. There will be a 60 minute break on subsequent playing days after the completion of 4 levels. Days 1A and 1B will play 10 levels. Day 2: Play will resume at 2:30 pm. The field will be combined and play 10 levels. Day 3 - play will resume at 2:30 pm and continue down to a winner or the completion of 10 levels, whichever comes first. Day 4 - if needed, play will resume at 2:30 pm and continue until a winner has been determined. If an event is running long, the tournament director reserves the right to suspend play after the completion of 10 levels and resume the following day. This event may take 4 playing days amd 5 calendar days to complete depending on field size.

$5,000 WSOP NO-LIMIT HOLD'EM STRUCTURE CHART

Following is the structure from a 2010 WSOP $5,000 no-limit hold'em tournament. For the $5,000 buy-in, each player receives 15,000 in starting chips.

LEVEL	ANTE	BLINDS
1	-	50-75
2	-	50-100
3	-	75-150
4	-	100-200
5	25	100-200
6	25	150-300
7	50	200-400
8	75	300-600
Remove 25 Chips		
9	100	400-800
10	100	500-1,000
11	100	600-1,200
12	200	800-1,600
13	300	1,000-2,000
14	300	1,200-2,400
15	400	1,500-3,000
16	500	2,000-4,000
Remove 100 Chips		
17	500	3,000-6,000
18	1,000	4,000-8,000
Remove 500 Chips		
19	1,000	5,000-10,000
20	1,000	6,000-12,000
21	2,000	8,000-16,000
22	3,000	10,000-20,000
23	3,000	12,000-24,000
24	4,000	15,000-30,000
Remove 1,000 Chips		
25	5,000	20,000-40,000
26	5,000	25,000-50,000
27	5,000	30,000-60,000
28	10,000	40,000-80,000
29	10,000	50,000-100,000
30	15,000	60,000-120,000
31	20,000	80,000-160,000
32	30,000	100,000-200,000
33	30,000	120,000-240,000
34	40,000	150,000-300,000

WSOP TOURNAMENT DESCRIPTION

Players begin with 15,000 in Tournament Chips. All levels will last 60 minutes. Breaks will occur after every two levels and last 20 minutes. Dinner break on Day 1 will be after the completion of level 6 and last 90 minutes. There will be a 60 minute break on subsequent playing days after the completion of 4 levels. Play will continue on Day 1 until the completion of level 10. Day 2: play will resume at 2:30 PM and continue down to the final table or the completion of 10 levels, whichever comes first. Day 3: play will resume at 2:30 PM, and continue until a winner has been determined. If an event is running long, the tournament director reserves the right to suspend play after the completion of 10 levels and resume the following day.

HOW MANY CHIPS DO YOU GET AT THE START?

Your starting chip total in a tournament is determined in advance by the tournament director. In low-limit events, a $30 buy-in might give you 500 in chips, though the tournament director could just as easily give you 200 or 1,000.

In 2009, the World Series of Poker started giving players triple chips for their buy-ins so that the tournaments would have more play. For example, in the main no-limit event of the World Series, you would get 30,000 in chips for your $10,000 buy-in. And in WSOP preliminary events that cost $1,000, you would get 3,000 in chips.

However, whether you are given 200 in chips, 1,000 in chips, or 10,000 in chips, you are on a level playing field with your competitors because in a tournament, everyone starts with the same amount of chips. It is up to you and your skill in playing, and how you work your luck, to see how far you make it into the tournament.

Unlike a cash game, where chips are the exact equivalent of money, tournament chips have no cash value. They may just as well be Monopoly money, because no one is going to give you anything for them outside the tournament. Thus, if you have accumulated 150,000 in chips and try to cash them out, all you'll get from the casino is strange looks and an explanation that all you have are tournament chips.

HOW IS THE TOURNAMENT PRIZE POOL DETERMINED?

The prize pool in tournaments is collected from the total amount of money put up by the players as entry fees. For example, if 2,000 players compete in a $1,000 buy-in event, there is $2 million available as prize money, less house fees and staff tokes taken out by Harrah's for the running of the tournament. In 2010, 10 percent was taken out of the prize pool for the $1,500 or less buy-in events, 9 percent for the $2,000 buy-ins, 8 percent for the $2,500 and $3,000 buy-ins, 6 percent for the $5,000 and $10,000 buy-ins, 5 percent for the $25,000 buy-ins and 4 percent for the $50,000 buy-in tournament.

The WSOP tournaments are set up so that approximately 10 percent of entrants will win cash prizes. For example, if the size of the starting field is 1,000, the top 100 finishers will win cash prizes. And if, like the Main Event, there are *thousands* of players, then there will be a horde of lucky winners. For example, if 7,000 players enter the Main Event, there will be 700 players coming away with winnings.

If you're fortunate enough to get to the final table of a World Series of Poker event, you will be in for a big haul, because that's where the big money lies. First place, of course, will be the biggest prize, followed in order by second, third, and so on, down to the last paid place, which usually returns what you paid to enter plus a little more.

The first place prize in the WSOP tournaments (as of 2010) is usually about 20 percent of the total prize pool, with the exact amount varying according to the tournament setup. It could be more, or it could be less, depending on how the prize pool is structured. Second place might get about 60 percent of the amount of the winner (about 12 percent of the total prize pool), with third place getting about 40 percent of the winner's share (about 8 percent of the total prize pool). That will account for approximately 40 percent of the prize money in the tournament. The rest of the prize pool is divided among the remaining winners, with the final table players getting more than players who finish lower down.

The payout structure will be posted soon after the tournament begins, as the organizers add up the total number of entrants and figure out the number of places and amount paid to each money-winner. If the structure will affect your decision to play, or if your curiosity can't wait the few minutes to the start time, you can approach the tournament director, who will have a good idea of the number of places to be paid. Most players simply wait until the tournament director makes the announcement and posts it on the television monitors that are typically placed in a location easily visible to the players.

You can judge whether an event is right for you by looking at the entry fee and the potential prize pool. The greater the number of players, the bigger the prize pool. If nothing else, you can always count on the Main Event at the WSOP to offer enough prize money that, should you win, you will be on easy street for the rest of your life.

In many of the big events, the prize pool often gets into the millions. These tournaments draw the top players you see on television, along with amateurs trying their hand at winning the big money. All you have to do is get in there and let fortune shine on you. Once the cards get dealt, you never know....

KEEP YOUR EYE ON THE TELEVISION MONITORS

The World Series of Poker strategically places television monitors in the tournament area so that all players can monitor the progress of the event. These monitors display the level of play, amount of blinds and antes, the number of places being paid, the amount awarded for each finish, and the blind and ante structure for the upcoming round. The fun part of these monitors is the **magic number**, the number of players remaining in the tournament after which, you're in the money. It is great fun to scoreboard-watch as the event progresses, seeing the number of active players dwindling as players get busted out. The *really* fun part is when you approach the bubble, and realize that if you can hang in there a bit longer, you'll make it into the money!

In every tournament there comes a point at which one more eliminated player will guarantee payouts for all remaining players. This is called being **on the bubble**. So if you're player number twenty-eight in a tournament that pays twenty-seven places, you've achieved the dubious distinction of being caught on the bubble. When you're the "**bubble boy**," you risk going home empty handed, while every remaining player fights on to go deeper into the tournament and win the bigger payouts.

TYPICAL TOURNAMENT RULES

At-Your-Seat Rule

The rules for the World Series of Poker tournaments state that you must be at your seat by the time all cards have been

dealt, for your hand to be valid, "at your seat" being defined as "being within reach or touch of your chair." If you're not, your hand will be considered dead. Players sometimes get up and stretch or wander over to other tables to check out the action, but if the cards arrive before you do, it's too late. The dealer will disallow play for that hand and collect your cards—hand over.

In the beginning of tournaments, when the tournament director announces to the players, "All players take their seats," and to the dealers, "Shuffle up and deal," you'll sometimes find delinquent players who will forfeit their blinds, sometimes for a few levels of play. Some well-known pros, most notably, Phil Hellmuth Jr., are notorious for showing up in big events hours after the tournament has begun. With the blinds relatively small in the first few rounds, tardy players can get away with losing a few chips since the blinds make only a relatively small dent in their stacks. Later on, however, when the blinds get large, these pros wouldn't dare take a long absence from the table because large chip losses could prove critical to their survival.

Some other rules and procedures apply to both tournaments and cash games.

Settling Disputes

Various disputes can arise during a game, either between players, or between a player and the dealer. If this occurs, ask the dealer to call over the "floor," meaning the floorman or tournament director, or call out for him yourself. Disputes are handled according to the established procedures. The staff will always follow the rules and try to be fair when interpretations are required. You can read the established rules for the World Series of Poker at www.WSOP.com.

Smoking Rule

Smoking is typically not allowed in the tournament area at any World Series of Poker tournament, so if you're a smoker, you'll have to head to the public areas of the casino or go outside to get your puffs.

Asking for Time

You are allowed to take extra time—up to a reasonable limit—during the play of a hand, a privilege you may want to use if you're faced with a difficult decision. Your opponents' remedies for undue deliberation, as well as yours if an opponent takes too long to make a decision, is to ask for the "**clock**." When a clock is called, the floorman will come over and give the deliberating player 60 seconds in which to make a decision, or his hand will automatically be folded. Any player at the table may call for the clock, even one not actively involved in the hand. When ten seconds remain, the floorman will countdown from ten so that the clocked player has advance warning that his time will expire.

Now that we've covered the basics of entering tournaments and how tournaments work, it's time to talk about one of the most important factors in your pursuit of winning a tournament. It's all about having the most chips at the end of the final day. The next chapter gives you the skinny on how the size of your stack influences your tournament strategy.

HOW YOUR STACK SIZE AFFECTS THE WAY YOU PLAY

It is not how you play your cards that counts the most—it's how you play your chips and your opponents. To be a winner in no-limit hold'em tournaments, you must accept this concept; every professional player intuitively understands and implements it. The number of chips you have relative to the big blind and the nature of your opponents are factors in *every* decision you make in a tournament.

Your chip stack influences so much of your strategy that you cannot afford to ever ignore it. In a tournament, it's all about the chips. When you're short on chips, you are under greater pressure to make moves to stay alive, and all your opponents are aware of this. When you're awash in chips, you can exert greater pressure on opponents who want to stay out of confrontations with you because you can wipe them out of the tournament. You have the luxury of choosing the spots that best suit your situation.

Let's take a further look at how the size of your chip stack affects *everything.* We definitely need to cover this important aspect of tournament play before we get into the next chapter on how to play at each stage of the tournament.

Why?

Because these concepts and definitions are the cornerstones of winning tournament strategy.

THE MINIMUM IDEAL STACK SIZE

Ideally, you would like your stack to be *at least* twenty-five times the size of the big blind. This is your **minimum ideal stack** size. You have enough chips to play pressure-free poker without worrying too much about being blinded out. Sometimes your chips get low and the pressure cooker is on the stove. Or worse, your chips might get really low and the situation becomes critical. Other times, you'll have a big stack, with leverage against smaller stacks that are just trying to survive.

CHIPS
It's all about the chips. Chips are survival. Chips are power. You need enough chips to survive, but you need lots of chips to prosper.

PLAYING SHORT STACKS

If you have less than ten times the big blind in your tournament stack, then you have a **short stack** and must play more aggressively to grow your stack. You don't have the luxury of waiting for good cards forever. By doing nothing but folding, every set of deals around the table costs you the equivalent of about two big blind bets. And if you're starting with only ten big blinds, one round means you're down to about eight big blinds and in two rounds you're almost cut in half and down to about six big blinds!

You can see where this is going. If you wait too long to make a move, you will soon get **blinded off**—lose all or most of your chips to the blinds and antes without even playing a hand! At the same time, when you have a short stack you are perilously close to getting eliminated from the action if you suffer one big loss. At the least, your stack will get crippled even more than it was.

The loss of leverage that you face as a short stack poses some additional problems:

1. Opponents give your bets less respect and are more likely to call you down with less than premium hands when you move chips into the middle. There are three reasons for this:

   a. They give you less credit for strong hands because they know that you have to make a move.

   b. You do not have enough chips to hurt your opponents, which minimizes your potential for bringing down the hammer—that is, putting a big intimidating bet in front of you.

   c. Being able to put the hammer to you gives your opponents the edge because they have a bigger stack and are only risking a few of their chips while you are risking your entire tournament.

2. Opponents are more likely to bet and raise against you. When your stack is desperately low, you may be forced to play all sorts of hands. Your opponents know this, so they'll be more likely to call your bets with weaker hands.

3. For all these reasons, it will be less likely that you can pull off a successful bluff.

PLAYING WITH EMERGENCY SHORT STACKS

Let's say that the antes are 25 and the blinds are 50/100 in a ten-handed game. You're sitting with 500 in chips. One round of deals goes by and you don't play a hand. Here is what happens: You lose ten antes at 25 each (for 250 total), plus a small blind at 50 and a big blind at 100. In just ten hands, 400 will be eaten up, leaving you 100—barely anything.

Obviously, you can't let this happen. You've got to make a play before that 500 in chips goes away. If you don't get chips quickly, you're a goner in one and half rounds of play, tops.

When your chip count is five-times the size of the big blind or less—what I call an **emergency short-stack**—you're in trouble. You must be ready to pounce with all your power at your very first decent opportunity. You have to pick up the blinds and antes to stay alive, as they are your food for survival. To give yourself the best chance of getting those chips, you must use all the leverage you have available. You cannot afford to play passively in this situation—calling is not an option, nor is a standard raise. The all-in bet is your *only* viable move.

Make a play before the blinds drop you a notch lower, and if possible, have a hand with some value to it. If the pot is unraised and you are dealt any pair, ace-anything, or any two cards 10 or higher, push in all your chips and hope for the best. Quite often you'll get no callers and the blinds and antes that you win will give you enough fuel for another round of play.

If a tight player or one who looks strong raises the pot in front of you, you might wait out a hand or two unless you think you have a better hand than he has. You're in survival mode and must pick a situation where you can win. The right situation means when you're holding the best hand and can win with the best cards. Or when you don't have the best hand but hope to win the pot without a fight. If you have to, make your move with *any* two cards. Keep this in mind: If you have 7-2 and go head-to-head against an opponent who has A-K, you're only about a 2 to 1 underdog. In other words, you always have a chance to take down the pot.

Don't forget you want to make your play while you still have some chips. This is extremely important. Better to play

7-2 with 500 in chips to win than 7-2 with only 100 in chips to win. In the first instance, you'll be up to 1,000 if you win, which will give you some more breathing room before you come hard at the pot again. And you will gain a little bit of leverage. In the second case, you will gain so few chips if you win that you won't improve your situation enough to really count. You still won't have any leverage.

You need chips and must make your play while you have something to win and while you have enough chips so that if your opponents buck heads against you, they have something to lose! The clock is ticking fast when you have an emergency low stack and you might get only one good shot. Just pick your best situation and go for it. You may have to go after the pot with any two cards. May the chips be with you!

WHEN THE ANTES KICK IN

The attrition is fast and harsh once the antes kick in and you're short-stacked. Every set of deals around the table costs the equivalent of about two big blind bets. Patience is no longer your buzzword. You're now thinking of *action*—in the right situation and at the right time.

With a short stack, you become more dependent on finding and taking advantage of the right situation because you have less time to wait for premium cards and big flops. You have to start taking more risks to get chips. This doesn't mean that you should play recklessly—that is never a good idea—but if the cards don't come, you've got to go out there and make something happen.

Winning pots if the right cards or situations come along, or stealing blinds or flops if they don't, should be right on top of your list. But like always, think *aggression*.

Beginners make the mistake of limping into pots with low stacks or calling all-ins with inferior hands. As a short stack, you want to make the big move *first* and put the decision to your opponents. Limping in with a third of your chips allows opponents to call with hands they may have folded against a bigger bet.

Make the big move when you have to make the big move. It's your only chance. By moving with *all* your chips, you maintain enough leverage to give opponents pause when considering whether to call your hand.

KEY TOURNAMENT CONCEPT
How you play your cards is not as important as how you play your opponents and your chips.

PLAYING AVERAGE STACKS

Having an **average stack**—about equal to the average amount of chips held by players, commonly called the **curve**—means that you're right in the center of things. You have enough chips to continue being patient and wait for your best opportunities. In other words, you can play your best poker without undue pressure.

Just like the big stacks, you want to avoid major confrontations against other average stacks or big stacks unless you believe that you have the best hand. Good players with chips will avoid confrontations with you as well, so you will have some bluffing opportunities. But again, don't lose chips by making foolish moves.

Smaller stacks are your targets. Push them around and get chips from them. If the big stacks are playing weak, don't be afraid to exert pressure on them as well. Look for chips wherever you can get them and from whoever will give them to you.

PLAYING BIG STACKS

Having a **big stack** means that you have more than double the average amount of chips in play. You have a big advantage as a big stack. You can afford to lose pots and still have plenty of chips to play, particularly against small stacks. This doesn't mean that you want to lose big pots, which can result from making a huge mistake or from taking a bad beat. It just means that you can afford a bad break and still be alive. You enjoy a luxury that smaller stacks do not have.

As a big stack, you can pressure players trying to stay alive by betting aggressively, especially against players who are playing scared or are short-stacked. You want to avoid other big stacks unless you think you have the best hand. This goes for average stacks as well, because a big confrontation with an average stack can make him the big stack and you the average one—or smaller.

Players fear big stacks, especially aggressive big stacks that are willing to push chips into the middle. When you sense weakness in an opponent, pounce on it. Stealing blinds, aggressive flop betting, and reraising are highly effective weapons. However, do not foolishly throw away chips just because you have a lot of them. Whatever good play got you the big stack, keep it going to maintain and increase your position. A big stack has leverage, but use that leverage wisely.

HOW TO EARN CHIPS WITH VARIOUS STACK SIZES

Take a look at this chart to understand a few ways that you can earn chips, no matter the size of your stack.

STACK SIZES		
Chip Stack	Stack Size	Strategy
Emergency Short	5x big blind	All-in first good situation.
Short	10x big blind	All-in is only bet.
Medium (Average)	Average stack	Play to style.
Minimum Ideal	25x big blind	Play to style.
Large	2x average stack	Step up aggression. Find opponents who play scared and pound them.

Now that we've covered the importance of factoring your stack size into your tournament strategy, it's time to learn the nitty-gritty strategies for winning tournaments. We'll start off in the next chapter by giving you tips on how to successfully navigate your way through the major stages of tournaments.

HOW TO WIN YOUR WAY THROUGH THE FOUR STAGES OF TOURNAMENTS

Chips are your lifeblood in tournaments. Everything revolves around how many you have. If you don't have any, you're dead, and out of the tournament. If you have a lot of chips, you're in very good position to finish near the top, or perhaps on top. And that is what it's all about.

Tournaments are designed to exert increasing pressure on players through blinds and antes that escalate at regular intervals. Fast tournaments, set up for one evening's play, may change the levels every 15 or 20 minutes, while big buy-in world-class events, like the World Series of Poker, have rounds of 60 minutes to two hours and are set up to last from two days to as long as ten days or more, as in the Main Event, the $10,000 buy-in no-limit hold'em championship.

All of these structures work the same way. Each level costs players more money in blinds and, after a while, antes, increasing pressure on them to make moves so that these forced bets don't destroy their bankrolls. If you sit out hand after hand, especially as you get to the higher levels, you'll go broke quickly if you're sitting there with short and medium stacks.

While your ultimate goal is to win the tournament, if you're able to get *in the money*, you will accomplish a tremendous achievement as a non-professional player. The higher you finish, the more money you get.

THE FOUR STAGES OF TOURNAMENTS

Tournaments can be divided into four stages: early, middle, late, and final table. Your goals throughout are to increase your chip count and, of course, survive to the next stage. While you would like to grow your chip stack after every round, you should not set artificial goals and force your play to get there. You can only do what you can do.

Have patience. Situations will present themselves but you have to be around to take advantage of them. The goals I set forth for each of the stages are only general guidelines to shoot for. Again, *que sera, sera*—what will be, will be. But to get to the end, you have to start at the beginning. Here is an overview of a tournament, stage by stage.

Let's start with the early round strategy.

Stage One

THE EARLY ROUNDS: SURVIVING AND BUILDING

In the first few rounds of a tournament, the blinds are small, and the antes often don't kick in until the third or fourth level. During these early rounds, with not much at stake, there is little pressure on you to make any moves or enter even one pot since losing your blinds won't make much of a dent in your stack, at least not a critical dent.

Your strategy in this stage is to play conservatively, trying to win little pots when possible and avoiding big pots and all ins unless you think you have the winner. You don't want to risk your tournament on a foolish bluff or by playing speculative or second-best hands for too many chips.

In these early rounds, you don't want to lose a significant portion of your chips or your entire stack trying to win a few hundred. Later, when the blinds are significant and you need the chips, you may take more chances in the right situations.

But early on, survive and wait for your trap hands. Still, you'll typically find at least one player who will go broke within ten minutes, even at the major championships. In fact, in a recent WSOP world championship event, a player lost his entire 10,000 in chips on the very first hand when he pitted his pocket kings against a player who made a full house on the river. That's exactly what you want to avoid.

Do you really want to have *all* your chips at stake in the beginning of a tournament with just a pair?

By the time the early rounds are over, more than one-fifth of the field will be gone. Your goal is to increase your chips stack as the tournament progresses. Hopefully you can double up after three rounds, but don't force the action. Play your cards and the situations—don't be driven by what you'd like to happen. If you've maintained an average chip count, you're still very much in the game. And that's a lot better than being very much out of the game.

Stage Two

THE MIDDLE ROUNDS: GETTING INTO POSITION

In the middle rounds of a tournament, around levels four to eight, players get eliminated at a more rapid rate. The blinds and antes start taking big chunks out of your bankroll, and each round of play removes more leverage from your stack. This means you need to take more chances to maintain the health of your chip stack and to avoid getting eliminated. For players whose chips have dwindled, the pressure is on and they have to start gambling to survive.

The middle stages are not just about playing defensively, but going on the attack. It is time to go after the blinds and antes more aggressively because there are more chips to be won. Build up your stack if you can. Chips are power, and the more of them you have, the better off you are.

Since no-limit hold'em is a game of leverage, you always want to make sure that you have enough chips in your stack so that when you make a bet, your opponents give it the respect it deserves. And if that bet is an all-in wager, it has to have enough weight to intimidate opponents and make them think very carefully about whether they want to call you. If your chip stack gets too low, your bets will scare no one. At that point, you have lost your biggest weapon in no-limit hold'em—intimidation.

Look out for players who are protecting their stacks. They're the ones to go after. If you are skillful enough and fortunate enough to trap an opponent and become one of the big stacks, the smaller-stacks will be wary of messing with you, giving you more opportunities to push players around.

If you're short-stacked, you have to steal blinds and play aggressive poker in order to keep up with the costs of blinds and antes. And if you get to a dangerous point—with a stack that is less than five times the size of the big blind—you need to look for opportunities to move all your chips into the middle. When you have a big stack, you want to push around the weak players and small stacks to gather more chips. You're looking to position yourself for the final table.

If you can survive these rounds, you're almost in the money. Many players will be eliminated during the middle stage, probably one-third to one-half the number who started, so you've made real progress. In the big tournaments, the $5,000 or higher buy-in events, you've also made it into the second day. Still, there is a long way to go.

Stage Three

THE LATE ROUNDS: GETTING IN THE MONEY

Tournaments become more exciting as the field narrows and you get close to being in the money. You have fifty players to go, then forty, then twenty. Suddenly, only ten more players need to be knocked out and you will be cashing at the World Series of Poker! Not only is that prestigious and a great accomplishment, it also means you've finished in the top 10 percent of all players.

You've won money and that's sweet. Bragging rights go with the territory. There is one more thing it means: you have a legitimate chance. Yes, you have a real shot at getting to the final table!

But let's go back to before you made it to that top 10 percent. If you've lasted into the later rounds, you've either made it into the money or are getting really close. Now you look forward, hoping to get to the final table and the *big* money. You want to pick up your game here and play your best poker. Avoid facing off in big pots or all-ins against stacks that can take you out— unless you've got the goods—but as always in a tournament, keep pushing your weight around against players that can be bullied.

WHEN YOU HAVE A SHORT STACK

First, if you're short-stacked and the blinds are eating you up, you have a tough decision to make. Do you go for it with an all-in move, or do you hold off, waiting for enough players to bust out so that you assure yourself of cashing? If you can hang tight, and it's only a few hands, why not wait and take the money? But if it looks like it will be awhile before the money hits, you're better off to make your move earlier if a strong opportunity presents itself. You've got to get your chips in the middle eventually, so you're better off with a good situation than a bad one. If you lose, you're out, okay. It is what it is. But if you win, you can coast, or if it suits your goals, you can get aggressive and try to accumulate chips.

WHEN YOU HAVE A BIG STACK

And that brings us to the bigger stack situations. If you have a decent sized stack, or even a big stack, you can bully the short stacks that are hanging on for dear life. You're thinking ahead—you're thinking final table—and you know that the more chips you have, the better your chances of getting there. If you win enough chips here, you can position yourself to make a good run at the big money. Short stacks will not want to tangle with you when they're so close, nor will medium stacks that don't need to take chances. With your bigger stack, you can take them out and end their dream—without their even getting a payday—so they're unlikely to get in your way.

No matter how you decide to play, your strategy will be based on your goals. Are you trying to cash first and worry about winning the whole enchilada later? Or is it, "Damn the torpedoes, full speed ahead?" Or possibly, "Let the chips fall where they may, I'm going for it now!"?

You decide. If you make the right decisions, and luck gives you a bit of a push (a helping hand, so to speak), you will make it to the final table.

Once you get into the money, you will win more prize money for every place higher you finish, or for every small number of places (usually table by table). You may want to fold marginal hands if lasting one or two more places means winning a lot more prize money. At the same time, if you are in a good situation, go for it. If you bust out, so be it. If you make a big play and win a basket load of chips, you've leapfrogged into position for a much higher finish. Really, when you start getting close, you've got to be thinking big.

Think, "final table, final table, final table." The power of positive thinking never hurts—and it just may keep you focused and help you get there.

Stage Four

THE FINAL TABLE: SHOOTING FOR THE STARS

You don't get to a final table very often, so when you do, you want to make the most of it. You have a good shot at winning it all, but you still have to get through the last players. Here are a few pointers on how to do that.

WHEN YOU'RE PLAYING IN THE BIG ONE

The "big one" at the World Series of Poker, i.e., the $10,000 buy-in Main Event, is the tournament every poker player dreams of winning. Fame and fortune await the skillful and lucky player who goes all the way. It could be you this year, but to get to the promised land you have to give luck every opportunity to come your way. The Main Event is different—and not just because it's the big one.

It's a **deep stack tournament**, which means that you start with a lot of chips and have ample time to make your moves. Therein lies your first directive: Take it slow. You have all the time in the world—at least, many hours—to wait for hands and situations that you like. Unlike some of the smaller buy-in tournaments, where you'll be blinded away if you don't dance quickly, the Main Event gives you plenty of opportunities to make moves.

The second thing to keep in mind is not to blow all your chips on a second-best hand. There's no need to push all your chips out there on an impulsive hunch. Sure, you may take down some chips, but if you run up against a monster hand, you're gone. And there's no coming back—at least not until next year. Maybe it wasn't bad luck that caused your demise—let's just hope that "mistake" isn't a better word for what happened.

Patience is the key. You've invested $10,000 for the dream. Are you going to let it go that cheaply? Sometimes, even when you think your opponent is bluffing, you're better off not getting involved deeply in a hand that you don't really *need* to play. Better to lose a few chips that won't hurt you than a lot of chips that will. In the Main Event, you'll have plenty of opportunities to find better places to take a stand.

IDENTIFY YOUR STYLE OF PLAY

You'll find a mix of amateurs, semi-professionals and professionals, many with different agendas and goals, at the final table. While it's safe to assume that most players at the table want to win the gold bracelet, the title means little to some people. Cash is their king. For others, creeping up one spot on the money ladder means paying the mortgage for a few months or putting their child through college. For others, anything short of winning the bracelet translates to failure. Determine what type of player you are. Be honest with yourself.

Are You Conservative?

Are you are the college-saving, mortgage-paying type? A very tight, let-everyone-else-bust-out style of play is a strong option for you—that is, if your stack size is large enough to allow you to sit back and play conservatively. Pay jumps are largest near the top, particularly at the final table, but you also can earn significant extra money by hanging on for a little while longer and letting other players battle it out.

Let's say that you fold nearly every hand for the first hour and two players bust out. You've just increased your winnings by 90 percent over ninth place—and you've paid for a college education, $75,084. Waiting through a few eliminations can really pad your bankroll. It can also do wonders for calming your nerves and getting you into your groove. After a few early bust-outs, maybe your patience will get rewarded with a big hand. Then you can decide whether you want to sit back a bit longer, or start playing a more aggressive style.

But beware. Playing conservatively can be dangerous, particularly if you start the final table with a short or medium stack. Your opponents at the final table will recognize what you're doing and mercilessly prey on your chips. While you are sitting back, the blinds and the blind stealers will start eating up your chips. If you choose a conservative style of play, only enter pots when you have the goods and aggressively play the pots you decide to enter.

Or is Winning Your Only Goal?

Winning the bracelet is all that matters to many players. They won't be sitting back, waiting for it to fall in their lap. If winning the title is your only goal, you are not limited to one particular strategy—do whatever you think you have to do to take it down. Continue to play the way you've been playing and hope that the skills and luck that have gotten you to the final table will carry you home. Remember, you don't have to bust everyone at the table to win the bracelet. Trying to do that often results in playing far too many pots, which can be disastrous. Be aware of your stack size relative to the rest of the field and the blinds, and use that information to help guide your decisions.

When You Have a Big Stack

If you're among the big stacks, avoid going to war against another big stack that can bust you or turn you into one of the small stacks—unless you're feeling really good about your hand. Use your big stack to put pressure on smaller stacks struggling to stay alive. Chips are weapons.

The blinds jump significantly at each level at the final table. A few loose plays and a blind increase and you're not so big anymore. Get an understanding of how the rest of the table is playing and exploit both the super-aggressive players and the passive, move-up-the-pay-scale type of opponents.

As the event gets down to four or five players, the play usually loosens up significantly. Short stacks are desperate and looking for their last chance to make a meaningful double up. If you have a big stack, be careful about over-committing. While the hand values for the lesser stacks will be weaker, your chips are too important at this point in the tournament to unnecessarily put them at risk. You don't get extra cash for being the one that busts the most players. The top money goes to the top finishers, however they get there. Play smart and you'll soon find yourself heads-up, money and bracelet sitting on the table, playing for a piece of poker history.

When You Have a Short Stack

In almost every tournament you'll ever play, there will come a time—and that time may be practically the entire tournament—where you're going to be short-stacked and under a lot of pressure. The key to surviving with a short stack is staying calm. Think before you make your moves, keeping in mind that every player eliminated means a huge jump in prize money for the remaining players.

When you're short-stacked, the blinds and antes are exerting tremendous pressure, leaving you with little choice but to find your best opportunity and then go after it for all your chips. Calling is not an option in this type of situation. Just be sure that you maintain enough chips to ensure that an all-in bet has **fold equity**—that is, your bet is expensive enough so that a larger stack does not consider it a trivial call. In other words, don't wait too long to make your move. Sometimes you must make a play to avoid becoming emergency-stacked. Put maximum pressure on opponents by betting all your chips on a preflop raise. If you have enough chips to sting opponents— and never let yourself get below that "sting" level—you'll make it hard for them to call, which gives you the best chance of walking away with the pot.

Don't give up. This does not mean that you can sit on your nest hatching eggs. With a short stack, you cannot afford to do that. However, it does mean that you should carefully choose situations where you make a stand. Wait patiently before committing all your chips to a pot that may be your goodbye hand. If you still have chips, no matter how tiny your stack, it can grow quickly. All it takes is a few double ups, then another double up, and before you know it, you're a player with real chips, maybe even one of the chip leaders. It can happen fast, and it often does. The key is that you must still be in action at the table, ready for luck to find you.

When You Have a Medium Stack

Playing a medium stack at the final table can be tricky. In fact, some pros think it's the toughest size of stack to play. The big stacks will not want to get involved with you—they'd rather beat up on the short stacks—yet they're the ones you can win the most money from. They also are the ones who can swiftly win all your chips in one hand.

The short stacks and the other medium stacks might be your best targets. But you can face problems with them too. If another medium stack beats you in a big pot, you'll join the ranks of the short stacks, or be crippled or eliminated if he's got more chips than you. So you've got to pick your situations carefully. When you go up against a short stack, you have less risk because an all-in loss here won't end your dream—though it will take a big bite out of your stack and consequently, your chances. It's better to hit the final table with a medium stack than with a short stack, though, in either case, the good news is that you're there, within reach of first place.

I suggest that you carefully observe the tendencies of the big stacks because they are ones that you can win the chips from. Many players who hit the final table with a big stack will sit back for a while and only get involved if they have to. This makes them prime targets for stealing the all-important blinds, which are your lifeblood if your medium stack begins to drift in the wrong direction. And only play premium hands against the short stacks, particularly if you have observed that they are tight. Come in with the goods and chances are good that you'll leave with the goods.

Don't let your stack get too short or a big stack might look you up. If you get too short, you might be forced to pick a hand, throw in your chips, and cross your fingers. That's the chance you take if you play a passive final-table style with a dwindling medium stack.

My best advice is to use a selectively aggressive style of play. Select your better hands to play, preferably in position against other medium stacks and certainly against the big stacks. Then play your good cards aggressively, yet wisely laying down your hand when you think you're beaten. Keep alert for opportunities to win chips and inwardly rejoice as each opponent gets eliminated, bringing you one step closer to victory.

When You're Heads-Up

When you get heads-up, you will usually be granted a short break before the play begins. Take advantage of it. Take a walk, get a drink, call your family, splash cool water on your face. Do what you have to do to prepare for what could be a long battle that lasts several hours.

Winning heads-up play depends heavily on psychology, so focus intently on how you've seen your opponent play and his personal demeanor at the table. Is he confident or reticent? Use your opponent's tendencies against him or her, and take down pots with well-timed raises, reraises and all-ins. Sitting back and waiting for premium hands isn't much of an option. Just ask Doyle Brunson—he won the world champion twice with a ten-deuce. That's right, a 10-2! Brunson has the uncanny knack of reading his opponents spot on, and choosing the right situations to make his moves. Timing is everything when you have only one opponent.

When that last river card falls on the felt and you take your first breath as a World Series of Poker champion, remember to acknowledge your opponent. He or she has just gone through the same ordeal as you, but fate happened to be on your side this night.

Your day has come! Bask in the sunshine of victory. And wave to your family and friends watching you at home on the tube.

Now, smile pretty for the cameras as they wrap that shiny gold bracelet around your wrist.

SEVEN THINGS YOU MUST DO TO SUCCEED IN TOURNAMENTS

To succeed in tournaments—and especially to make it to the final table—you must put seven important skills into your game plan. These are the main ingredients of your recipe for success. Throughout this chapter, I reiterate one primary concept: aggressiveness. Playing your good hands aggressively is essential to a winning style of play in tournaments.

THE 7 KEYS TO SUCCESS

1. Surviving
2. Winning Chips
3. Playing Without a Hand
4. Minimizing Bad Plays
5. Using the Power of Chips
6. Knowing When to Back Down
7. Playing Aggressively

1. SURVIVING

Basic tournament strategy boils down to one thing: survival. That's right, *survival.* Your goal is to hang in there and move up the ladder as other players get eliminated. You want to get into the prize money. And finally, you want to get to the final table and win the tournament. You must carefully pick your spots, ones that you can win, so that as players get knocked out of action, you remain in the thick of things. As the weak get separated from the herd, you will continually climb closer to the top of the ladder.

Patience and concentration are integral to survival. You cannot afford critical lapses in judgment. Throwing all your chips into the pot on a foolish bluff or recklessly chasing with a drawing hand are two of the worst plays you can make. In a cash game, you can always go into your pocket for more chips if you get broke. Not so in a tournament. You don't get a second chance. And that's why you must be patient and wait for your spot to pounce.

If you hang around long enough, you give good situations a chance to find you. Good cards and good situations will come along. Just make sure you're still around to take advantage of them. World champion of poker Tom McEvoy calls it "giving yourself a chance to get lucky." He should know: McEvoy defeated nineteen other world poker champions to win the inaugural Champion of Champions tournament at the 2009 WSOP.

2. WINNING CHIPS

You must have chips. Without enough of them, you have little to win when you catch big hands and everything to lose in confrontations with a bigger stack.

When good hands and situations come your way, you want to have chips, lots of them, so that you can win big pots. Maybe you'll get dealt pocket aces or kings, get action on them, and see your hand hold up. Perhaps you'll flop a set, or make an even bigger hand, and be able to trap an opponent who loses to your boss hand.

But you always need enough chips to take advantage of your primo hands. If you have 1,000 in chips and trap an opponent, the most you can win from him is 1,000. But if you have 7,000 in chips, you have a lot more upside potential.

To maximize your chances of success in no-limit tournaments, you need leverage. Chips give you that all-important edge. When you have enough of them, your opponents will fear your bets. And of course, you will survive longer. You never want your chip stack to get so low that you lose the power of the hammer or the ability to win enough chips if you go all-in for your entire stack.

To paraphrase a popular commercial, "Got chips?" If you do, build them. If you don't, get them.

3. PLAYING WITHOUT A HAND

You don't get dealt a lot of good cards in no-limit hold'em, so you need to occasionally make moves without strong hands. Look for situations where you can outplay opponents and steal their chips. Be ready to push opponents off a pot with a big bet and no cards to back it up. It's called a bluff. It's the beauty of poker—and life. You fluff your colorful feathers and hope they don't get clipped.

Players who sit and wait for good cards before they play hard don't go far in a tournament. Their play will be predictable to their opponents, and their opportunities to gather chips will be few. No-limit hold'em is a situational game. When you sense weakness, use your chip hammer and pound your opponents with it. Take an opponent off a pot and take his chips. In other words, play the player.

Of course, when I say that you can win chips without a hand, I don't mean it in a literal sense—although T.J. Cloutier won a hand without cards in a road game years ago. T.J. calls this true story the day that he won with his "mystery hand."

Seems he was playing in a cash game in Texas with a group of friends and rounders, one of whom often dozed off during the game and never looked up when he was in a hand. T.J. was sitting to the immediate right of the dealer and the dozer was sitting to the dealer's left when they played a pot heads-up.

T.J. decided to move all-in against the dozer, but just as he started pushing all his chips to the middle, the dealer mistakenly slid his cards into the muck. T.J. gently moved his cupped hands back in front of him as though he still held cards. With his head still bowed, the dozer tossed his cards into the muck and the dealer awarded the pot to T.J. Everybody else at the table saw what had happened and got a good laugh out of it.

4. MINIMIZING BAD PLAYS

No-limit hold'em is a game of mistakes, as T.J. has said over and over again in the many poker books he has written. The player who makes the fewest mistakes wins the most chips.

You must minimize bad plays, particularly catastrophic ones that can cripple your stack and set you back into the trouble zone. You could even lose the whole enchilada on one bad play. Taking that walk of shame out of the poker room, all the while beating yourself up about how stupid you were in making such a bad play, is not a happy occasion.

Sometimes you'll play correctly and lose. That's okay. Bad beats are a part of the game and you can't worry about them. It's when you know that you're the only one to blame for bombing out that you can really take a guilt trip. Just be sure not to cripple your chances of surviving and possibly winning by playing a hand that you shouldn't have played in the first place. Minimize catastrophic plays and you maximize your chances of making a final table—or better. How do you do that? Discipline, my friend, discipline. Maintain your patience. Wait for the right hand or the right situation.

Chips are a limited resource and you can only replenish your supply by winning more of them. In no-limit, your entire stack of chips is subject to risk and loss at any time. So when you do push the big stack of chips in the middle, you want to be fairly confident that you have the best of the situation, that the odds are stacked on your side—and not on your opponent's side of the fence.

5. USING THE POWER OF CHIPS

In a tournament, chips are power, chips are your life blood. If you have a lot of them, take advantage of your superior chip count by bullying short stacks and timid players with aggressive play. Anytime you go to battle against a smaller stack, he knows that if he goes to war with you for all his chips and loses, he will be eliminated. It is difficult for short stacks to play back at you because you can break them. Conversely, when you're that smaller stack, you must tread carefully against bigger stacks because your tournament will be at stake if all the chips go in the middle.

At all times, and certainly before you go into battle, know your opponents' relative chip status. Who's got the big stack? Who has an average stack, and who's on a short stack? And determine how your stack stands in the pecking order.

You need to know which opponents you can bully because you have the dominant stack, and which ones can bully you because they have the dominant stack. If you're the loser in all-in situations against a bigger stack, your tournament life is over. However, if your stack is more sizable then your opponent, all you can lose is chips—you'll still be alive to see another hand. Never underestimate the power of chips.

> **TIP**
>
> When you have fewer chips than an opponent, he can take you out if all the chips get in the middle and he wins the pot. When you have more chips than your opponent, you can take him out.

6. KNOWING WHEN TO BACK DOWN

Making good laydowns is one of the most important skills in poker. You have to know when to back down from a hand that you think is pretty good—but might not be the best—and give up the pot. It doesn't matter how good your hand is. It only matters whether it is *better* than your opponent's hand. As Doyle Brunson has so often written, it doesn't take a big hand to win—it just takes the best hand.

But you have to know when to fold 'em as well as when to hold 'em. You must have the guts to lay down a big hand against a lot of betting pressure. Players who don't heed warning signs take big hits in cash games and suffer early exits in tournaments.

If it looks like you're in big trouble on a hand, don't be afraid to let your cards go. Don't get married to your hand. Marriage may not last forever, but death does. Remember that bets saved are the same as bets won. Folding is one way to save your bets—and sometimes, your tournament life.

7. PLAYING AGGRESSIVELY

Aggressive betting gives you two ways to win pots: Either your opponents will back off the pot and give it to you, or they call and get pounded even harder on the next card. If they call all the way to the river only to find out that they've been butting heads with a monster, they're in trouble. That's a chance most players will not be willing to take unless they're fairly certain they have you beaten.

Winning is always about aggression. Bets and raises make opponents think before messing with you. And it makes them think about folding. Advantage: the player betting and raising. Disadvantage: the opponent watching you collect his chips.

But you cannot play aggressively in every situation. Sometimes it takes more finesse than aggression to win a pot. That's why the pros advocate playing selectively aggressive. First they select their spots—with either the best hand or the best situation—and then they come out swinging.

No matter how you play, you must have enough leverage to go the distance. The next chapter gives you valuable tips and insights on how to build your leverage in tournaments.

SEVEN WAYS TO INCREASE YOUR LEVERAGE IN TOURNAMENTS

Having more leverage than your opponents is key to winning tournaments. What gives you leverage? Chips, chips, chips. In tournaments, you not only need to win chips to keep up with the steady erosion of your stack caused by the constantly increasing blinds and antes, you need them to keep up with the increasing number of chips held by the average player as the field thins.

Tournaments start with a set amount of chips, and from start to finish, the total number of chips in play neither decreases nor increases. It remains constant—it's just that fewer and fewer players hold them as their competitors get eliminated and their chips get spread among the players still in action.

For example, if you start out with 1,000 in chips in a field of 100 players, 100,000 total chips are in play. If 50 players get eliminated, the average stack doubles, with each player averaging 2,000 in chips. Of course, some will have more, and a few many more, while some will have less and others will hover on the brink of elimination with emergency low stacks. But there's still that same 100,000 total chips in play. If you've remained static at about 1,000, you're behind the curve, which denotes the size of the average chip stack.

So, your fate is not just about keeping up with the blinds and antes so that your stack remains constant. You need to grow your stack. Of course, you can't force the action and increase

your chips just because you want to. You can only do your best given the circumstances and cards that present themselves. If you're behind the curve, opportunities will come along to gather more. Hopefully, you will prevail in those opportunities and win some chips. Unless you're short-stacked and have to make a big move, patience is a virtue. You've got time—use it to your advantage.

These are the main strategies you can use to win chips and increase your leverage in no-limit hold tournaments:

1. Stealing Blinds (and Antes)
2. Restealing
3. Betting the Flop
4. Taking Advantage of the Bubble
5. Using the Hammer
6. Setting a Trap
7. Playing Aggressively

1. STEALING BLINDS AND ANTES

Stealing blinds and antes on the preflop is the bread and butter of your hold'em arsenal and a great way to replenish your chip stack. Without picking up other players blinds, you're going to have a hard time surviving. You need those chips to replenish your own loss of chips to the blinds and antes. You don't get many good hands to play, so while you are waiting for good cards to come your way, you need to occasionally steal blinds holding nothing—in other words, on a pure bluff.

The best positions to steal blinds from are the button or the cutoff seat. Use the power of late position to raise three times the size of the big blind (or more), and hopefully force the blinds and later position players out of the pot. Often, the blinds will fold, giving you the pot uncontested. You don't want to make this play every time you're in late position, because your opponents will catch on and spank you back with a reraise that forces you to fold. But if the blinds are going to give you the pot without a fight, well then, take it every time.

2. RESTEALING

Late position players, and sometime even middle or early position players, will try to steal the blinds. When you get a good feeling that your opponents are just going after the blinds, make a pot-sized reraise. If they are on a steal or playing a weak hand, they'll fold and give you the pot. That's called a **resteal**. It's a bolder play than the steal because it requires you to put more chips at risk, and there's always the chance that your opponent has a legitimate hand. But in poker, that's always true. Anything could occur, nothing is for sure. You can't play scared and hope to win at no-limit hold'em.

The resteal puts lots of pressure on your opponent and gives him plenty of reasons to fold. When it works, it's even better than the steal because you have won not only the blinds, but your opponent's raise as well.

3. BETTING THE FLOP

Aggression, aggression, aggression—again that's the key to success. Betting and raising win chips. Take the lead and come out betting on the flop. More times than not, that pot will be yours. But don't overuse this play to the point that everyone knows you're going to make the move. If you become too predictable, aggressive opponents will come over the top of you and take your chips away in a New York minute.

Going after flops aggressively, no matter what three cards appear, will win you many pots, especially against tight players. Not so much against loose players. If you know that your

opponent will call you no matter what you do, be careful how you play against him.

4. TAKING ADVANTAGE OF THE BUBBLE

Everyone wants to win money. And everybody wants the prestige of finishing in the money in a tournament. But to do that, you first have to make it past the bubble. When you're close, you don't want to be the player who busts out on the bubble with the money going to everyone else. Nobody wants that to happen to them.

As a result, play slows down and almost everyone starts playing very conservatively, just waiting for one small stack to bust out. That is, *almost* everyone. Actually, the bubble presents a golden opportunity to stockpile chips. So, if you have enough chips to play with, one spot away from the pay table is the time to step up your game and steal and resteal while the rest of the crowd hangs on to clear the bubble.

5. USING THE HAMMER

Big bets and all-in bets put a lot of pressure on smaller stacks. Even the bigger stacks feel the pressure of big-bet poker. No player ever wants to lose a big pot, especially the smaller stacks that will go bye-bye if they play for all their chips and lose. Use the hammer to pound your opponents with the big bet at the right times, and you'll take chips away from them.

If opponents fear that you will wield your hammer, they'll be more likely to get out of your way even when you just tiptoe into the pot. Look up your weak opponents and blast away at them with aggressive bets that they'll have a hard time calling. Yes, be merciless. You're not in the tournament to make friends, just money.

6. SETTING A TRAP

You can win some huge pots in no-limit hold'em tournaments by trapping an opponent. The best time to set a trap is when you get a big hand and your opponent also has a big hand, but one that is not as strong as yours. For example, suppose you hold aces against an opponent's kings, and all the chips find their way into the middle before the flop. It's hard for the average player to fold a hand as strong as kings, though I've seen it done. In 1999 at the Tournament of Champions, David Chiu, the eventual winner, laid down pocket kings preflop when Louis Asmo raised all-in. Chiu realized that pocket aces was the only hand his opponent would risk his entire tournament with. And he was right. Asmo turned them up after Chiu folded.

Another time when you can spring a trap is when you have a huge disguised hand against an opponent who has no clue that you're holding a monster. Get as many chips into the pot as you can in this type of situation. You might be up against an aggressive player who pushes his luck too far, or one who thinks he's leading your horse to the water, not realizing that you're holding a big hand and that the oasis is yours, not his.

Sometimes you're fortunate and all the chips get in the middle without much work. Other times you have to be sneaky. And the right cards have to drop so that your opponent will believe that he still has the best hand. You have to figure out how best to shake the coconuts from your opponent's tree— and hopefully all of them.

But to set the most effective trap, you need to have enough chips to win a lot of chips. And hopefully your opponent also has enough chips to really make the hand a windfall for you.

A trap situation will show up for you—if you're still around to take advantage of it. Hands don't come when you're on the rail, nor do they help you much when you don't have enough

chips to win much. The key is this: Don't panic and go out on bad hands just because you're running cold and feel like you need to make a big play. Hang around, good things will happen.

7. PLAYING AGGRESSIVELY

There's that word again—*aggression*. To win at poker, particularly at no-limit hold'em, you have to be aggressive. The worst thing you can do in no-limit tournaments is turn into a **calling station**—you know, the player who calls bets and rarely raises. Reread the first six ways to increase your leverage in tournaments. What single element do they all have in common? You guessed it—aggressive betting.

The player who wins the chips is usually the player who goes after them. And he's the player who will eventually build the most leverage in the tournament.

KEY CONCEPT
YOU WANT TO BE BLUFFED!
It is better to be wrong by folding and get bluffed out of some chips than to be wrong by calling and get eliminated from the tournament.

A big part of your success in building your leverage and winning your way to the top depends upon how well you can read your opponents, that is, how correct you are in predicting their responses to your actions. If you raise, how likely is your opponent to reraise? Is he more or less likely to call or to fold? In the next chapter, I'll give you some proven ways to predict the actions of your opponents in no-limit hold'em tournaments.

HOW TO PREDICT THE ACTIONS OF YOUR OPPONENTS

No-limit hold'em is not so much a card game as it is a people game. No matter what your cards, you always must play them against people. No-limit hold'em is about psychology, trying to deceive opponents about the strength of your hand or the lack of it, while at the same time trying to ascertain the strength of theirs. It is about inducing opponents to either fold when you bet so you can win the pot right there, or getting them to put more money into a pot you believe you'll win.

Deciding the best way to play a hand depends on how you predict your opponents will react to your checks, calls, bets and raises. Part of your thinking process includes determining how you think they think you're going to react to their betting actions. That's how it works at the poker table—while you're trying to figure them out, they're trying to figure you out.

Spy versus spy.

In other words, it's all about playing the player. Learning how to adjust for various types of players is a key ingredient to winning tournaments. You predict that Steve will act in a certain way, so you adapt your strategy accordingly to take advantage of him. And, oh yes, take his chips too.

Now let's look at two important keys to predicting the actions of your opponents.

#1. CAREFULLY OBSERVE YOUR OPPONENTS' PLAYING TENDENCIES

Observing an opponent's playing tendencies—conservative or aggressive, loose or tight, big bluffer or not a bluffer—is obvious to everyone regardless of their experience. Whether a rank beginner or a seasoned expert, any player can quickly and easily see whether an opponent plays a lot of hands or only a few, and whether he tends to call or raise.

At the table, it doesn't take long for a player to reveal his playing style. And once you have an idea of your opponents' styles, you can adjust your own play to maximize your results. Playing styles can be categorized into one of four fundamental types—conservative, aggressive, loose, and tight. There are substyles as well, but these main categories will give you a general sense of the types of opponents you'll face. Let's take a closer look at them.

FOUR TYPES OF PLAYERS

1. Loose Players

Loose players love action. They play too many hands, call too many bets, and stay in pots too long. By playing more hands, they will win more pots, but at the expense of too many bets when they lose. Net result: overall losses—unless they're a world class player who can get away with this type of play. Since loose players play more hands, their cards will be weaker, on average, than your typical non-loose opponent. So you need to adjust.

PLAYING AGAINST LOOSE PLAYERS

When you're in pots against loose players:

1. Call more often at the showdown, since they'll get there with weaker cards.
2. Don't try to move them off of pots when you have nothing. Bluffing just won't work against players who'll call with any hope in their hand.
3. Play more marginal hands than usual when you're heads-up, since their average hand will be weaker. However, stick to a fundamentally solid approach. Don't get drawn into a loose player's game.

Let loose players win their pots. You like to see that. The more they win, the more chips they have for you to win later on. When you're doing battle against them with a big hand, you'll make them pay a hefty price for playing weaker cards to the end.

2. Tight Players

Tight players enter few pots and only with premium hands. Against them you need to loosen up your game. Play more aggressively against tight players since they'll more readily give up the pot. When you bet or raise them, they'll usually fold marginal hands. This means you can easily push them out of pots with any garbage you hold—your cards are irrelevant when an opponent won't defend his hand. When you're playing hold'em, particularly no-limit, you'll want to consistently attack their blinds, which they won't defend.

PLAYING AGAINST TIGHT PLAYERS

Take advantage of tight opponents by always figuring them for a good hand when they're in the pot. Respect their bets; they're generally betting on solid cards. In borderline situations, give tight players the benefit of the doubt and call their bets less often. When you do call their bets, call with cards you figure can win. And if a tight player raises, make sure the pot odds and the strength of your hand justify a call, because he probably has cards worth betting on.

Since tight players won't play mediocre hands, you can force them out of the pot early with strong bets. If your hand is mediocre and a tight opponent bets, give him credit for strength and save your chips. Note that tight players can be either conservative or aggressive.

3. Conservative Players

Conservative players play non-aggressive poker—tending to call rather than raise and check rather than bet. They put little pressure on opponents. This style of play tends to be very predictable and keeps the level of risk relatively low for their opponents. In Texas hold'em, you need to protect your good hands so that the field is narrowed, and your good hands hold up to be winners.

The advantage of playing against conservative players is that you get to see more cards for free or at least cheaply. Marginal hands are more valuable because you'll be able to see more cards with them, and if you hit your hand, you're going to win chips you'd otherwise have no shot at. Conservative players make big mistakes when they let opponents into a pot when they should be shutting them out. The more hands an opponent lets you sneak in on, the more vulnerable that player is to having pots taken away from him—sometimes, big pots.

PLAYING AGAINST CONSERVATIVE PLAYERS

In general, you want to up your aggression against conservative players. Aggressive play will allow you to more frequently drive conservative players out of pots even when you have inferior hands because they are less likely to defend pots unless they have strong cards. If they happen to be playing behind you, steal their blinds by raising every time they let you. No-limit hold'em is the wrong game for conservative players.

If you're lucky enough to get in hands against these kinds of opponents, you'll get extra opportunities to win chips.

4. Aggressive Players

Aggressive players keep the heat on during a game. They bet and raise frequently, so getting involved in a hand with them is going to cost you chips. Aggressive players take advantage of opponents' tendencies to fold rather than put more chips into the pot, and they'll keep pushing at pots with hands that don't support such heavy betting.

PLAYING AGAINST AGGRESSIVE PLAYERS

When you mix it up with aggressive players, you know they're going to pound you with bets and raises, so you must be ready to commit chips if you're going to play a pot against them. To counteract their style, you have to fight fire with fire and be prepared to raise their bets, or reraise their raises. If they've got nothing, which will often be the case, you'll be able to take that pot. Of course, you have to make good reads when you're committing chips because aggressive players won't always have nothing. But at the same time, you can't let players push you around.

Aggressive players will throw lots of chips around, so slowing down your game when you get a big hand can pay big dividends. An aggressive opponent will build the pot for you while your passive slowplay disguises the strength of your hand.

#2. DETECT OPPONENTS' TELLS: LEARN THE BODY LANGUAGE OF POKER

The body language, expressions or mannerisms that reveal the strength or weakness of a player's cards are called **tells**. Tells are subconscious mannerisms that are telltale signs you can use to your advantage There are two types of tells—the physical ones described below, and betting pattern tells. A betting pattern tell reveals information on the quality of a player's hand. You can often determine how strong or weak his hand is by the amount that he bets and under what circumstances he bets, calls or raises.

10 TELLS YOU CAN TAKE IN, BUT SHOULD NOT GIVE OUT

There are tons of tells, some that are common among novice players and others that are particular to individual players. It is always important to carefully observe your opponents, not just for their style of play and betting tendencies, but for tells that can help you determine the best way to play against them. Here are ten basic tells that will help you get an edge on opponents.

1. Players who act strong are often weak, a concept first discussed by Mike Caro. Players talking loudly or betting in an aggressive manner would like you to believe that they've got the goods. Conversely, players who act weak are often strong. As above, look for opposites. Watch out for a player who looks like he is reluctantly tossing his chips into the middle. He's got a strong hand.

2. Players who grab their chips as if they're going to bet while you contemplate your betting action. They're trying to intimidate you into not betting if you're leading into the action—or not raising if a bet has already been placed—so that they can come into the pot for free or at least, cheaply. Or, if they have led out with a bet, for you to fold.

3. Players who look at you when they bet or even stare you down. It's an intimidation tactic to get you to fold or not bet. Think item #1 on this list; acting strong when weak.

4. Players who look at their chips when new cards are revealed on the board. Subconsciously, they're thinking about the chips they want to bet, meaning they've got a hand worth betting on, probably a strong one.

5. Players who look at the pot when new cards are revealed. Ditto above. They're subconsciously counting chips for a pot they figure to win.

6. Players who watch your chips while awaiting your betting action. They're nervous about a potential bet from you because they're weak.

7. Player who are unnaturally quiet when they're in a hand. Look for strength.

8. Players who appear more nervous or excited than usual when they're involved in a hand. They're not nervous because they have a weak hand, but because they're strong!

9. Players who appear to be frozen after betting and are awaiting an opponent's reaction. They're bluffing.

10. Players that look at their cards again often don't remember what they have. What does this mean? Their cards are not that strong or they would remember.

Note that while most tells are the real deal, some players may consciously show a fake tell in an attempt to fool you. So don't put 100 percent faith into tells because they are not always reliable. Always use your poker knowledge and intuition as the main guideline for making strategy decisions. If you think you have a tell on an opponent, use that to influence your decision but only if you're more than reasonably certain that the tell is legitimate.

Tells can provide valuable information, especially against beginning players and at low-limit tables, but like every other decision in poker, always consider all the information at hand before you choose an action. The classic book on tells, *Caro's Book of Poker Tells*, is required reading if you want to learn more about how to predict your opponents' actions.

16 TWO WAYS TO EARN YOUR TOURNAMENT BUY-IN ON THE CHEAP

Don't have enough spare change for a buy in to the tournament your want to play? Not to worry—you can get in the old fashioned way: Earn your buy-in.

How?

Win a satellite. Satellites are great values because they give you the chance to gain entry into a larger buy-in tournament for a fraction of the cost. The two major types of satellites are one-tables and **megasatellites**. You only have to compete against nine other players in a one-table satellite, but they cost more to enter than the megasatellites. A **megasatellite** is a lower buy-in tournament featuring multiple tables. The top finishers win an entry into a large buy-in tournament. Technically, the WSOP will issue a **lammer,** a chip that is equivalent to the buy-in for the big tournament you were playing for. You may use that lammer for a tournament entry of the equivalent cash value, or trade it in for cash.

This chapter gives you pointers on two ways you can earn your way into a tournament via a satellite: winning your tournament seat in a one-table satellite at the WSOP; and winning your seat in a WSOP megasatellite.

Of course you can also win your entry fee by playing in a **side game** (cash game) during the WSOP. Juicy cash games with various blind structures are played 24/7 right around the clock during the World Series of Poker. We've already covered

winning strategies for no-limit hold'em cash and tournament games, so let's move right along to how to play one-table satellites.

1. PLAY WSOP ONE-TABLE SATELLITES

One of the best ways you can earn a seat in a big tournament is by winning a one-table satellite. Just be careful about how many of them you enter, as even the best satellite players expect to win only one out of four satellites they enter, but that doesn't mean they won't go ten satellites without winning even once! There is a lot of variance in tournaments, and with luck being a factor in the short run, it is not uncommon to run hot or cold. Therefore, I suggest that you set up a satellite bankroll in advance to keep yourself from spending more money for satellites than it would cost to enter the tournament you want to play.

The one-tables move at a fast pace. The rounds are 15 to 20 minutes long, and the satellite usually lasts for only an hour or two. As quickly as possible, you need to learn how to play against each player at your table. You only have a short time to do this, so you must carefully observe your opponents from the get-go

These four tips will help you quickly identify the nature of your opponents:

1. Which players are conservative?

> **Tip:** They're the ones you can run over. Intimidate them with aggressive play. If several of your opponents are timid, all the better.

2. Which players are aggressive?

Tip: Pick your spots carefully, but when a player bets and raises too often, they're open to having pots taken away from them with a big raise. But be careful about betting in to them.

3. Who likes to play a lot of marginal hands?

Tip: Loose players can be tricky to play against after the flop because it's hard to put them on a hand. So, why not try to get rid of them preflop by putting in a raise to take their chips for free? Also, since they play weaker hands, you can too. If you can see the flop cheaply, you may be able to outplay or outdraw them after the three cards hit.

4. Who does not usually defend his blind?

Tip: Aggressive play will open the door for you to steal a timid player's blind. If they're going to give you the blinds, then why not take them? Just don't overdo it. If you steal too often, the timid player just might bite back.

Now that you clearly understand the types of players you must defeat to win your seat, you have to do the deed. You have to play your best game to do that. Ask yourself these five questions before you enter a pot. Your answers will be critical to your success in the satellite.

1. How strong is my hand?
2. Am I in good position at the table?
3. How many chips do I have compared with my opponents?
4. What is the dominant playing style of my opponents?
5. How soon will the limits rise?

Always keep your eye on the clock so that you know how much time is left in the round. The clock is important because it often becomes a major factor in how you play your cards.

Short Stack Tips

When you're working with a short stack in a satellite, the clock is even more important. If the limits are about to increase or you'll have to post the blinds on the next two hands, you need to either play a hand or look for a good situation to win some chips, especially from a tight opponent.

Don't ever despair when you are short on chips. Think of your stack as being one bet. You only have to win one all-in hand against an opponent who has three times your number of chips to double up and get even with him. In fact, if a player has exactly a 3 to 1 advantage over you in chips, you're only two hands away from breaking him.

Big Stack Tips

If you have a big stack, smart, aggressive play can build your chip count and make you stronger. But there are situations in a satellite when you can achieve great results by changing up your play. One way to do that is by sometimes slowplaying a big hand. For example, if you think that an aggressive opponent will raise if you just limp into the pot, you can trap him with a check-raise. You can also slowplay by checking on the flop against an aggressive player. You hope that your check will entice him to bet so that you can come over the top of him. The idea is to get as much money as possible into the pot so that you can build your stack and eventually win the whole enchilada.

Never Give Up

Two or three players usually get busted out in the early rounds of satellites. If you're a good satellite player, you know how to quickly adjust to the changing conditions as the table gets shorter and shorter. In fact, strong players can adjust their play well enough to make it to the top even when the table is short-handed and their stack is also short.

When Brad Daugherty started playing heads-up for the championship at the final table at the 1991 WSOP, he was at a terrible disadvantage to his opponent. "I was heads-up at the championship table with Don Holt, who had about 2 million to my approximate 200,000," Daugherty said. "At that point all I was doing was looking for hands to double through with, and then double through again. Fortunately for me I was able to double through to approximately 400,000, then to 800,000, and then to 1.6 million."

The rest is history. He became the first person to win $1 million in the Main Event at the WSOP. His advice is: "Don't give up when you are behind, just look for hands that you can double up with. Pretend you're chopping down a tree with an axe—one chunk at a time—until it falls down."

2. PLAY MEGASATELLITES AT THE WSOP

The megas at the WSOP are structured to give you plenty of play. For example, a $300 buy-in (plus a $30 entry fee) megasatellite starts you with 2,000 in tournament chips. For every $10,200 generated through buy-ins, one seat is awarded into the WSOP championship event. The tournament withholds approximately 10 percent from the total buy-ins for administration fees and the staff. You'll find the structure sheets for WSOP megasatellites below.

Daugherty's come-from-behind success story at the 1991 WSOP final table is as good as the solid advice on winning a mega that he and Tom McEvoy wrote in their seminal book on how to win satellites, *Championship Satellite Strategy*. In the book, the authors compared a mega to a football game.

"Megasatellites are similar to football games in that they have four quarters of play. The first quarter of a super satellite consists of the first three levels of play and is the rebuy period. At the end of this quarter, the super satellite truly begins. The second quarter is composed of levels four through seven, when you're trying to stay alive and accumulate some chips. The third quarter includes levels eight, nine, and ten (depending on the number of players in the event), when you are jockeying for position. The fourth quarter is the final table play."

MEGASATELLITE
NO-LIMIT TEXAS HOLD'EM

STRUCTURE SHEET		
$300 Buy-In + $30 Entry Fee, $500 BUY-IN + $50 Entry Fee		
LEVEL	ANTE	BLINDS
1	—	25/50
2	—	50/100
3	—	100/200
— 15 Minute Break		
4	25	100/200
5	50	200/400
6	75	300/600
7	100	400/800
Remove 25 Chips 15 Minute Break		
8	100	600/1,200
9	200	800/1,600
10	300	1,000/2,000
11	400	1,500/3,000
Remove 100 Chips 15 Minute Break		
12	500	2,000/4,000
13	500	3,000/6,000
14	1,000	4,000/8,000
Remove 500 Chips 15 Minute Break		
15	1,000	6,000/12,000
16	2,000	8,000/16,000
17	3,000	10,000/20,000
18	4,000	15,000/30,000
Remove 1,000 Chips 15 Minute Break		
19	5,000	20,000/40,000
20	5,000	30,000/60,000
21	10,000	40,000/80,000
22	15,000	60,000/120,000

The most important thing to remember when you're playing a mega is that you don't have to win it to earn a seat. That's right—you don't have to place first. Multiple seats are awarded based on the size of the prize pool. For every $10,000 in the prize pool of a mega at the WSOP, one seat will be awarded. For example, if the prize pool is around $50,000, the top five finishers will win a seat for the championship event.

In that case, if you're one of the chip leaders among the last six players at the final table with only five seats up for grabs, you might find yourself doing some unusual things to survive long enough to win your seat. You might even fold premium hands such as pocket aces or kings before the flop. Yes, sometimes that's the correct play because all you care about is one of those five seats; winning is irrelevant. In fact, once that extra player is eliminated, the megasatellite is over and the seats are awarded.

The competition is tough when you've gotten that far. So, if an opponent who has only about half as many chips as you decides to move all-in before the flop, your best play may be to fold those two cowboys you're looking down at. Why gamble on losing the seat you already have locked up? If you call his raise and lose the pot, he will catch up with you. Why take that chance? You can avoid that kind of risk if you just concede the pot to him.

If you're playing a medium or a short stack, you may find that it is easier to steal from a player who has a lot of chips than from an opponent with a short stack. Why? Because the big stack may be protecting his chips and is more likely to throw away some premium hands that the short stack is sure to play. The big stack probably doesn't want to play against somebody who plays bad and thus risk losing his precious chips if they wind up beating him with trash. So, if you're short-stacked, you can use that knowledge against him and go after his big stack.

Very late in the satellite, it's often "move-in or move on" when you have a short stack. Large stacks are basically taking turns stealing the blinds, while the short stacks are waiting to go all-in when they find a hand to play. Finally, somebody wakes up with a hand and calls a short stack's all-in raise. And that is usually how short stacks bust out, thinning the field and hastening the end of the satellite.

Now, suppose you're just a few seats away from getting into the money. The play changes at that point in the megas. Everybody starts playing survival tactics. This is when you need to know which players you can steal from, as well as those who never allow you to steal. You're looking for players who are hanging on, posting their blinds, and waiting for somebody to get broke so they can move up a notch. Go get 'em!

Playing in a mega is a great way to get tournament experience if you're fairly new to big buy-in tournament play. You can often learn some of the cheapest, yet most important, lessons of your poker career by swimming with the big fish in the smaller pond of a mega before you try going upstream against them in the Main Event.

TIPS ON MANAGING YOUR TOURNAMENT BANKROLL

BE SMART WITH YOUR MONEY

Being smart with your money is the key to becoming a winning no-limit hold'em player. You must exercise sound money management principles and have emotional control to handle the ups and downs. Riding a winning streak too hard or betting wildly during a losing streak are just two of the many ways that players beat themselves. But you don't have to make mistakes like that if you follow these three basic principles:

1. Only enter tournaments you can afford and that are comfortable for you.
2. Don't play when you're not at your best. If you're exhausted, annoyed, or simply frustrated by bad hands, players or life in general, take a break. The WSOP runs tournaments every day during the championships, so there's always another tournament coming around the bend.
3. Never play with money you cannot afford to lose, either financially or emotionally. Risking funds you need for rent, food, or other essentials is foolish. The short-term possibilities of taking a loss are real, no matter how easy the tournament may appear.

This is sound money management advice. Follow it and you can never go wrong.

Let's begin with the most important concept for all players:

> ### Never gamble with money you cannot afford to lose, either financially or emotionally.

The short term possibilities of taking a loss are real, no matter how easy the game may appear, no matter how stacked the odds are in your favor. Just as poor players don't always lose, good players don't always win. If that were not the case, losing players would never play poker because there would be no hope of winning, and good players would have no one to play with. There are ups and downs in any gambling pursuit, whether you're highly skilled, or a rank beginner.

Any one player can beat any other player during a poker session. That's the fun of the game. There are good days and there are bad days. It's just that better players will have more good days than bad days and will make money in the long run, while less skilled players will have more bad days than good days, and will end up losing money over time.

Whether you're playing tournaments or cash games, the most important thing is to stay within your comfort zone and play at levels you can afford. Always play at limits that won't stress you out or put you in a vulnerable position. If your rent money is due, pay the rent before you enter a tournament. If you have important bills, get them covered before you play. You should only gamble with discretionary funds, extra money that you don't mind putting at risk and potentially losing.

How much should you risk? Again, it is about your comfort level. Big players like Doyle Brunson, Daniel Negreanu or Johnny Chan can lose $250,000 in one day because it won't ruin them financially. It's a normal swing for the stakes they play and the risk they are accustomed to taking on. Presumably, you don't have that kind of money to lose or the skills to play that high, so this wouldn't be appropriate to you. The point is, if it hurts to lose money—either emotionally or because you're strapped for cash—you shouldn't be at the poker table in the first place.

If you're smart with your money, you'll lose your table bankroll at the worst—that is, the exact amount you planned on risking before you hit the tables—and at best, you'll make a bundle of money and have a great time doing so. It's a simple truth: If you never play over your head, you can never get into trouble.

Find a tournament where you feel comfortable with the stakes, one where the betting range fits your temperament and emotional makeup. If larger buy-ins make your heart pump too hard, you're over your head and need to find a game with lower ones. When you play with what poker players refer to as "scared money," you can be easily bullied and pushed away from your optimum playing style. To win, you must go into the action with every asset you have, so you can't give your opponents a way to push you around because the stakes are too dear for you.

Remember that poker is a form of entertainment and must be kept in that perspective. If you are preoccupied with losing money and it creates undue anxiety, its entertainment value and probably your winning expectation will slip rapidly. If that's the case, take a breather, recoup your confidence, and then hit the tables with fresh vigor. Recognizing that emotions affect the quality of play is an important step in making poker an enjoyable and profitable experience. Play only with that winning feeling.

This brings us to a very relevant question: How much should you put at risk?

Let's take a look at bankrolling.

WHAT IS YOUR BANKROLL?

There are two types of bankroll requirements for poker: table bankroll and total bankroll. **Table bankroll** is the amount of money you bring to the table and risk losing in any one session. **Total bankroll** is the amount of money you set aside to help you weather the inevitable losing streaks that occur in any form of gambling. Table bankroll is an irrelevant concept when it comes to freezeout tournaments, since once you buy in, you can't reach back into your pocket to by more chips like you could in cash games (or rebuy events which are no longer offered at the WSOP). So we'll just discuss total bankroll requirements here.

How do you figure out the size tournament you can play given your bankroll? Simple. First decide how much money you're willing to put at risk. If the limit you would like to play is too high for your bankroll, you can't afford it. Find another, cheaper tournament. And if you're budgeting for several tournaments, or a bunch of them, make sure you can afford the buy-ins in case you get shut out of earnings on all of them.

If the $1,000 buy-in tournaments are too high for your budget, than try to get in through the satellites and megasatellites run by the World Series of Poker. Look at it this way: If you want to play at higher levels than you can currently afford, then you'll need to earn your way to the higher limit by winning at a lower level.

For example, let's say that you have $300 to play with and you want to enter the $10,000 buy-in Main Event. Obviously, you don't have nearly enough, but you could stretch for the extra $30 and try one of the $330 megasatellites. With some good fortune, you may earn your seat! And if you are successful in the big one, well, you won't have to worry about entry in the following year's Main Event, will you?

KEY CONCEPT
Being undercapitalized in poker—or in business—virtually dooms your chances from the start.

Your total bankroll requirements will vary by the size tournament you want to play, however, the following guidelines will help you determine the proper amount to put at risk.

YOUR TOTAL BANKROLL

If you casually play poker with friends once a week or in cardrooms as a recreational activity, you don't need to be so concerned about a total poker bankroll, just what you're willing to risk in that one game. You can look at it as an allowance for your Friday night or once-in-a-while game.

However, if you plan on playing a World Series of Poker tournament, you need to have enough money set aside to be able to afford to lose your buy-ins in their entirety. Only 10 percent of all entrants make it into the money, which means, on average, you will win cash only one in ten times. That's on *average*. You could just as well lose fifteen tournaments in a row. Poker players call this *variance*, and it is a fact of life in tournaments.

Remember, no matter how good you are as a player or how weak the level of competition, you can't always win. If you take a tough loss in one tournament, hey, it happens. Take a breather, catch some fresh air, and come in to the next tournament with new energy and the feeling of a winner. You should only play a tournament when you're feeling fresh and brimming with confidence.

You almost have to look at tournament play as if it were baseball and you were a hitter. Good baseball hitters only average hits three times in every ten at bats. That's a 70 percent failure rate. And those are the best ones. Poker tournament are tougher. Average tournament players will cash only once in ten times, which is a 90 percent failure rate. The point is, you have to take failure in stride. It is part of the game.

TOURNAMENT BANKROLL REQUIREMENTS

In tournaments without rebuys or add-ons, you can only lose your entry fee. Not a penny more. So it is very easy to figure out your bankroll limitations.

If you plan to enter tournaments on a regular basis, you need to figure out how much you can afford. While you can only lose a certain amount in one tournament, you can lose an unlimited amount by playing an unlimited number of tournaments. If they're small entry fee tournaments, you may not give too much thought to their cost, except of course, if you're on a tight budget. You can look at these expenses the same as other types of entertainment—a ballgame, concert, or movie.

But if you plan on playing the World Series of Poker events—the $1,000 or even the $10,000 (or more) entry-fee tournaments—you need to map out a budget to determine whether you can afford the costs. Sure, it's nice to dream of hitting it big, but don't let the dreams turn into nightmares. You must manage your money to guide you through the dry spells.

The reality of tournaments—and this is very unlike the cash games—is that long, dry spells are common when the fields are large. It is not uncommon to find many top players being shut out from cashing in *any* of the events played at the World Series of Poker championships—and there are over 50 events played. You have to look at the big picture before putting your money at risk. Set your limits before you get into action, and strictly follow the guidelines you've planned out *beforehand.*

PLAY TOURNAMENTS ONLY WHEN YOU FEEL LIKE YOU CAN WIN

As we've discussed earlier, wins just won't be there every day. Once you get it through your head that you can't win every time, you'll be able to accept losing and get comfortable with this concept so that the times you do lose, which will be the vast majority of times you play tournaments, you can come back fresh for the next tournament.

But if you've lost that winning feeling, slow down. Take a breather from tournaments or side games. Even the best tournament players in the world take an occasional hiatus to refresh their minds and their spirits.

Only play when you are feeling confident that you can win. It's hard enough to win when you're at your best, why jeopardize your chances when you're not at your best or are playing scared poker. You've got to feel well to play well.

Part 4

LOOKING BACK AT THE WSOP: 40+ YEARS OF EXCITING GROWTH AND GOLD BRACELETS

by Dana Smith

"We had eight players last year, and this year we had thirteen," World Series of Poker founder Benny Binion said in 1973 at the end of the fourth annual WSOP, held at the iconic Binion's Horseshoe in downtown Las Vegas. "I look to have better than 20 next year. It's even liable to get up to be 50, might get up to be more than that. It will eventually."

Binion's prophecy has come true in spades: The 2009 WSOP at Harrah's Rio Hotel and Casino attracted 60,875 entries with 6,494 players in the championship event.

It would take three decades before poker became accepted as a respectable profession, but even then Binion believed that the game could be promoted as a competitive sport. A visit to the Reno Holiday Hotel a few years earlier had strengthened his faith in his innovative idea. Tom Moore, owner, and Vic Vickrey, casino promoter, had invited a group of Texas gamblers and a few deep-pocket "producers" (losing players with large bankrolls), to attend a loosely organized event they called a Gaming Fraternity Convention. They set up a couple of poker tables in a corner of the casino and "tossed in $3,000 of the hotel's money just so's these fellas would have a little somethin' extra to try shootin' at," Binion said.

Doyle Brunson, the "Godfather of Poker," was there: "Moore found out to his dismay that pretty much all we wanted to do was play poker, and he didn't get enough action at his

more profitable games, like blackjack and craps. So when Jack Binion asked him if he was holding the convention the next year, Moore figured it wasn't worth the trouble. But Jack and Benny figured it different. When Moore sold his business, they used that tournament as a springboard for what they thought was a grand idea: a World Series of Poker that would be played at their Horseshoe casino in downtown Las Vegas."

It all began in 1970 when the Binions invited a few of their big players to sit down for a social tournament at the Horseshoe. At the end of the five-game event, the poker players voted Johnny Moss the champion of poker. And that's how World Series of Poker was launched. Like a snowball running downhill for the past four decades, it has become the world's premier poker sports event.

ROAD GAMBLERS DOMINATE THE WSOP IN THE EARLY DAYS

Though today's WSOP is professionally produced and smoothly administered, everything about the first years of the World Series of Poker was amateur except the players—they all were professionals, most of them Texas road gamblers, migrant workers who plied their trade in smoky backrooms nestled along the dusty back roads of the Southern poker circuit. No events were actually scheduled and no one was formally invited, the word simply got around.

"If seven 7-card stud players arrived at the Horseshoe at the same time, they'd play the 7-stud contest, provided one of them wasn't asleep," Eric Drache, director of the WSOP in the early days, observed in one of the early WSOP brochures. Johnny Moss added, "In those days it warn't no one game an' it warn't no freezeout. You had to win all the games, win all the money. Then you're the best player, an' they vote on you. I win all five games that year an' they give me a big trophy. In '74 they give me this here gold bracelet with the date engraved on the back. I win a silver cup, too—solid silver, engraved."

Most of the road gamblers traveled to the early WSOP mainly to play in the high-stakes side games, as well as enter a tournament or two. Satellites were nonexistent until 1983, when Tom McEvoy became the first satellite winner to win the Main Event. Satellites opened the doors to expansion for the Series: Before then, few players who had not traveled the Southern poker circuit or played in the big games in Texas and Louisiana entered the WSOP tournaments.

In 1971 Binion changed the WSOP format to a process of elimination, primarily because it hadn't captured the attention of the media. The World Series of Poker didn't have a series of competitions that included a big play-off at the end and awarded a hefty prize to the winner, as in other sports. In 1972 he upped the buy-in for the no-limit hold'em championship tournament to $10,000, which has remained the same over the years.

The plan worked—Amarillo Slim Preston's victory at the 1972 World Series of Poker triggered an avalanche of national media attention. With his gift for gab, the tall toothpick from Texas was a natural-born promoter who went on to make eleven appearances on Johnny Carson's *Tonight Show*, and had three stints on *60 Minutes*.

THREE CHAMPIONS WIN TWO IN A ROW

In 1974, at the age of 67, Johnny Moss became the first three-time winner of the championship event at the WSOP. Stu Ungar repeated Moss' feat twenty-three years later in 1997 when he won the Main Event, sixteen years after his repeat wins in 1980-81. Only two other WSOP champions have won back-to-back titles: Doyle Brunson in 1976-77 and Johnny Chan in 1987-88. Coincidentally, both Brunson and Chan almost won three championships each, Brunson when he placed second to Ungar in 1980, and Chan when he was runner-up to Phil Hellmuth Jr. in 1989. Brunson is one of the few poker players to have a two-card hand named for him. He won both Main Events with a 10-2 starting hand, which has become known as a "Doyle Brunson."

The first year for which complete figures for the World Series of Poker were available was in 1977. The prize money of $806,800 was awarded to a total of 366 entrants into the twelve preliminary tournaments and the championship event. The first ladies-only WSOP tournament, a seven-card game, also was played in 1977, and the victor was awarded $5,580. Today the ladies' event is no-limit hold'em and the prize is over $1 million.

SATELLITE WINNERS AND AMATEURS SWELL THE FIELDS

In a shocking upset at the final table of the Main Event in 1979, California advertising executive Hal Fowler defeated well-known Texas professionals Bobby Hoff, Johnny Moss and Crandell Addington to become the first amateur to win the World Championship of Poker. The next amateur to win the title was Michigan accountant Tom McEvoy in 1983. By the conclusion of the 2009 events, fifteen people who were amateurs at the time they played the tournament—student, farmer, attorney, chiropractor, business owner—had won the WSOP championship. McEvoy also made WSOP history as the first player to win his seat in the Main Event via a satellite.

Today, satellite tournaments are a primary portal into the WSOP preliminary tournaments and the Main Event.

The championship tournament drew more than 100 entrants for the first time in 1982, when Jack Straus defeated 104 players for $520,000. By 2006, the number of entrants in the Main Event had escalated to a record 8,773 when talent agent Jamie Gold won the title and $12 million. The 1990 world champion of poker, Mansour Matloubi from Wales, became the first citizen of a country other than the United States to win the Main Event. Since then, the World Series of Poker has become an international happening. In 2009, players from 115 nations participated in WSOP tournaments, including Joe Cada from Michigan, who won the world championship of poker.

STU UNGAR WINS RECORD THIRD TITLE IN 1997

It was a scorcher on Fremont Street in Las Vegas by the time Stu Ungar and John Strzemp got heads-up for the championship duel on the outdoor stage at the 1997 WSOP. Gabe Kaplan sat in the commentator's box with ESPN cameramen toting equipment the size of Mac trucks that emitted enough heat to cancel out the steam misters carefully installed underneath the poker table for the players' comfort.

Although the spectators and press that crowded into the sweaty bleachers enjoyed the thrill of watching Ungar's return to the area after his seventeen-year hiatus from poker, mercifully, the duel in the sun ended after only six hands. Ungar raised before the flop with A-4 and Strzemp called with A-8. The A-5-3 flop maintained Strzemp's lead, but it also gave Ungar a gutshot straight draw. When Strzemp bet, Ungar moved all in and the casino executive pushed his last chips to the middle.

Ungar won his third championship title when a deuce fell on the river to complete his ace-to-5 straight.

This dramatic finish was not the first time that Ungar had won the title by making a gutshot wheel on the final hand. In 1980, the brash, young rookie played heads-up with the legendary Doyle Brunson and hit a wheel card on fourth street to break Brunson, depriving the "Godfather of Poker" of his third championship title.

Regarded as the greatest tournament player in the history of poker, Ungar used his uncanny reading ability and perfectly timed moves to carve his name into WSOP history and legend when he made an unparalleled comeback from near obscurity to win the title on a steamy spring day in 1997. It was the last time most people ever saw him play. A year later, The Comeback Kid died at the age of forty-five.

THE WSOP HITS THE BIG SCREEN IN 1998

The 1988 championship event is a classic in World Series of Poker history, in part because Johnny Chan won it for the second consecutive year, but primarily because the final hand he played against runner-up Erik Seidel was featured in the 1998 movie, *Rounders*, starring Matt Damon as a frustrated college student who travels to Las Vegas to play in the "biggest game in town."

When the final hand began, defending World Champion Chan had 1,374,000 in chips and challenger Seidel had only 296,000. They both entered the pot for the minimum bet. The flop gave Chan the nut straight and Seidel a pair of queens. Chan bet a modest 40,000. Not suspecting a trap and playing beyond his experience to get this far in the tournament, newcomer Seidel raised 50,000 with top pair. The crafty Chan flat-called. The turn card was an innocuous deuce and Chan checked his unbeatable hand. Deceived by Chan's underbet on the flop and his check on the turn, Seidel pushed in all of his remaining chips. The impotent river card changed nothing, and Chan won the championship of poker for the second year in a row.

Now a respected poker professional who has won eight WSOP gold bracelets, Seidel gave interviewer Dana Smith his take on his intriguing 1988 match with Chan. "It was surreal to find myself heads-up with Johnny at the final table. I was pretty bad in those days, especially shorthanded," he said. "I remember looking at the whole scene, the lights and cameras and all those chips, and thinking, 'What in the world am I doing here, playing heads-up for the world championship?' It was pretty awful to be in such a great spot and to be so unprepared for it. Still, it was the most incredible experience—to play for four days and get heads-up with Chan—just knowing that I could do it, that I could play at that level."

Matt Damon and Ed Norton, the stars of *Rounders*, actually played in the 1998 WSOP to promote their movie. When an *Entertainment Tonight* reporter asked the pair how they fit in with Doyle and Slim and "some of these old characters," Damon answered, "I don't know that we did." Norton added, "We're skinnier than most of them."

MONEYMAKER MAKES HISTORY IN 2003

Playing in the biggest Main Event field to that date, accountant and amateur poker player Chris Moneymaker defeated 838 competitors in 2003 to win the World Championship of Poker. An overnight celebrity, Moneymaker quickly made the rounds of the talk shows, including David

Letterman, and his intriguing rags-to-riches story appeared in major print media around the world. Thousands of casual players regarded his victory as proof that if an amateur like Moneymaker could make $2.5 million playing poker, so could they.

The unassuming and personable Moneymaker is widely credited with providing the spark that led to the rebirth of poker in walk-in casinos and the vast popularity of televised poker events.

OWNERSHIP OF THE WSOP TRANSFERS TO HARRAH'S IN 2004

From 1970 until 1998, Jack Binion and his father Benny had run the show at the Horseshoe on Fremont Street. In 1999, Becky Binion Behnen acquired ownership of the legendary casino and its world-famous tournament in a family financial arrangement. Falling upon hard times in her efforts to keep pace with the modern casino industry, the Binion heiress sold the Horseshoe and the WSOP to Harrah's in 2004.

Since then the tournament has grown significantly each year, from 13,036 total player registrations for all tournament events in 2004, to 58,720 in 2008. That year, the WSOP awarded $180,774,427 in prize money. According to a December 2007 article in *The Economist*, poker is the third most watched sport on cable television, following the NFL and NASCAR. The WSOP also has expanded its tournaments internationally with the guidance and professional leadership of Harrah's Entertainment. The first-ever WSOP event held outside the U.S. took place in September 2007 in London at the Casino at the Empire in Leicester Square.

THE BATTLE OF THE BRACELETS

No sporting event would be as compelling without its rivalries, its hotly contested races to the finish line, its contests of strength against cunning. Along with a cash prize, tennis awards crystal or silver trophies to its champions; football gives a gold ring to each member of the team that wins the annual Super Bowl; racing awards silver cups. The World Series of Poker, the richest sporting event in the world, rewards its world champion with a cash prize typically in excess of $5 million, plus a coveted gold bracelet.

Bracelets have become synonymous with titles at the WSOP—an easily identifiable status symbol of excellence in the ever-expanding world of tournament poker. The first gold bracelet was awarded to Johnny Moss at the WSOP in 1974, the year he won his third world championship title. Since that time, the bracelet award ceremony has lived on to become the defining moment in a poker player's career.

Today, the winner of each WSOP tournament with a buy-in of $1,000 or more wins the first-place money in that competition, plus a highly prized gold bracelet. To signify the prestige of winning the Main Event, Harrah's Entertainment awards a custom-designed gold bracelet encrusted with diamonds to the winner of the signature world championship no-limit hold'em $10,000 buy-in tournament.

One eventual world champion described his awe at playing against poker champions during his early tournament career: "No sooner had I placed my bet than five bracelets almost beat me into the pot. Talk about intimidation!" Later in his journey to the top of the poker world, he joined the ongoing race to see who could win the most gold bracelets.

In 2006, after a two-year epoch during which poker's three most famous players—Doyle Brunson, Phil Hellmuth and Johnny Chan—had been locked in a virtual dead heat with

nine gold bracelets each, Johnny Chan won a record tenth WSOP gold bracelet

Chan's lead in the battle for the bracelets lasted less than a week. In media director Nolan Dalla's account, "Four remarkable days after Johnny Chan won his tenth WSOP title, Doyle Brunson returned to poker's center stage. In front of an SRO crowd and a barrage of ESPN television cameras, Brunson rewrote the record books one more time when he won his tenth gold bracelet." His tying win came in the $5,000 six-handed no-limit hold'em tournament. As the gold bracelet was fastened to the 73 year-old champion's wrist, a reporter asked how it felt to still be able to compete at poker's highest level. "It's hard to substitute for experience," Brunson said. "No one has more poker experience than I do. Then again, no one here is as old as I am!"

And certainly not the man who broke the 10-bracelet deadlock, a player who is one of only three people to win three gold bracelets at the WSOP within a single year—Phil Hellmuth Jr. Coming into the 2006 WSOP, Hellmuth lagged one bracelet win behind Brunson and Chan. In one of the final tournaments preceding the Main Event, he finally broke the barrier that had separated him from winning membership into the exclusive "Ten Win" Club with a victory in the $1,000 no-limit hold'em with rebuys event. And with that, the three-way race to win gold bracelet number eleven was on.

It was short. And it was very sweet for Hellmuth, who won the $1,500 no-limit hold'em event the next year in 2007 to become the first and only member of the "Heavenly Eleven" Club. Not only did Hellmuth win his record eleventh bracelet, he won it against the largest field he had ever conquered, 2,628 entries, in his 38th WSOP final-table appearance.

"I honestly would have paid a million dollars for this moment," Hellmuth told a cheering crowd afterward. "I'm maybe the best hold'em player in the world, at the top of my game, and I felt it would be a shame if I didn't win the bracelet." As the crowd faded and he walked away from the staging area, Hellmuth whispered one final question to the tournament director. "So, how much money did I win?"

And that just seems to be the way it is at the World Series of Poker. First the bracelet, then the money.

PART 5

 **HOLD'EM GLOSSARY**

Ace-Anything:
An ace with any other card.

Act:
To bet, raise, fold, or check.

Active Player:
Player still in competition for the pot.

Add On:
Purchase additional chips in an add-on tournament.

Add-On Tournament:
A tournament that allows players a final purchase of additional chips.

Ante:
Mandatory bet placed into the pot by all players before the cards are dealt.

Average Stack:
In a tournament, having about equal the average number of chips held by players.

Bet:
Money wagered and placed into the pot.

Big Blind:
The larger of two mandatory bets made by the player two seats to the left of the dealer button position.

Big Pair:
A pair of jacks, queens, kings, or aces.

Big Cards:
Two non-paired cards jack or higher.

Big Slick:
The A-K as starting cards.

Big Stack:
In a tournament, having more than double the average amount of chips in play.

Blinded Off:
In a tournament, having lost all or most of one's chips to the blinds and antes without playing a hand.

Bluff:
To bet or raise with an inferior hand for the purpose of intimidating opponents into folding their cards and making the bluffer a winner by default.

Board:
The face-up cards shared by all players. Also Community Cards.

Bubble:
In a tournament, the point at which all remaining players will win money except for the next player eliminated.

Bubble Boy:
The unfortunate player who goes out on the bubble, missing out on the prize money.

Button:
The player occupying the dealer position who goes last in all rounds except the preflop; also the disk used to indicate this position.

Buy-In:
A player's investment of chips in a poker game or the actual amount of cash he or she uses to "buy" chips for play.

Call:

To match an amount equal to a previous bet on a current round of betting.

Calling Station:

An unflattering term for a player who calls too many bets and rarely raises.

Card Protector:

A chip or small ornament used to indicate a hand is live and protect it from getting fouled.

Cardoza's 4 & 2 Rule:

A simple formula to figure out the approximate chances of winning a hand by multiplying the number of outs on the flop by four and on the turn by two.

Cardroom Manager:

Cardroom supervisor in charge of the poker games.

Cash:

To win money in a tournament; currency used instead of chips to play poker or with which to buy chips.

Cash Game:

Poker played for real cash money (as opposed to a tournament).

Check:

The act of "not betting" and passing the bet option to the next player while still remaining an active player.

Check and Raise:

A player's raising of a bet after already checking in that round.

Chop:

To divide the pot equally with one or more players as a result of a tie between winning hands.

Clock:

If an opponent takes too long to make a decision, any player may ask for the "clock." When a clock is called, the floorman will come over and give the deliberating player 60 seconds in which to make a decision, or his hand will automatically be folded.

Community Cards:
The face up cards shared by all players. Also Board.

Conservative Player:
A player who tends to call rather than raise, and check rather than bet.

Correct Odds:
A situation in which there is a long term expectation of breaking even or making a profit.

Cowboys:
Pair of kings.

Curve:
In a tournament, the average amount of chips held by players.

Cut Card:
A special colored plastic card that is not part of the deck that is used specifically for the purpose of cutting the cards.

Cutoff Seat:
The seat immediately before the button.

Dealer:
The player or casino employee who shuffles the cards and deals them out to the players.

Deep Stack Tournament:
A tournament that starts with a lot of chips and gives players plenty of play.

Early Position:
Approximately the first third of players to act in a nine- or 10-player game or the first or second to act in a six- or seven-handed game.

Emergency Short Stack:
In a tournament, having less than five times the size of the big blind bet.

Face Down:

A card positioned such that its rank and suit faces the table and cannot be viewed by competing players. Cards dealt this way are also known as Downcards.

Face Up:

A card positioned such that its rank and suit faces up and is therefore visible to all players. Cards dealt this way are also known as Upcards or Open Cards.

Fifth Street:

The river; the fifth board card.

Final Table:

In a tournament, the last table of players.

Flop:

The first three cards simultaneously dealt face up for community use by all active players.

Flush:

Hand containing five cards of the same suit.

Flush Draw:

Four cards of the same suit needing one more card to form a flush.

Fold:

Get rid of one's cards, thereby becoming inactive in the current hand and ineligible to play for the pot.

Fold Equity:

A bet that is expensive enough so that an opponent does not consider it a trivial call.

Four-of-a-Kind:

Hand containing four cards of identical value, such as 9-9-9-9, four nines.

Free Card:

A betting round where all players have checked, thereby allowing players to proceed to the next round of play without cost.

Freeze-out Tournament:

A tournament in which players may not purchase additional chips—once they lose their chips, they're eliminated.

Full House:

Hand consisting of three cards in one rank and two in another, such a 7-7-7-Q-Q.

Hammer:

In no-limit, a big intimidating bet or raise or the threat of one.

Hand:

The cards a player holds; the best five cards a player can present.

Head-to-Head:

Hand or game played by two players only, one against the other. Also Heads-Up.

Hole Cards:

Card held by a player whose value is hidden from other players.

Image:

How a player's betting and playing style is perceived by his opponents—for example tight, loose, conservative, or aggressive.

Implied Odds:

See Potential Gain.

In the Money:

To win a cash prize in a tournament.

Late Position:
The last two or three seats in a nine- or 10-player game, or the last or next-to-last in a game with five to seven players.

Level:
A specified period of time in a tournament, marked by increased blinds or antes.

Limit Poker:
Betting structure in which the minimum and maximum bet sizes are set at fixed amounts, usually in a two-tiered structure such as 5-10.

Limp:
Call a bet as a way to enter the pot cheaply.

Loose Player:
A player who plays too many hands and stays in pots too long.

Magic Number:
The number of players remaining in the tournament after which, players are in the money

Main Pot:
The original pot in a hand where a side pot is formed due to a player running out of chips.

Medium Pair:
A pair of eights, nines, or tens (and sometimes sevens).

Medium Stack:
See Average Stack.

Middle Position:
Approximately the second third of players to act in a nine- or 10-player game or the third or fourth to act in a six- or seven-handed game.

Minimum Ideal Stack:
In a tournament, having at least 25 times the size of the big blind.

Money Management:

A strategy used by smart players to preserve their capital and avoid unnecessary risks.

Muck:

To fold.

No-Limit:

Betting structure in which the maximum bet allowed is limited only by the amount of money the bettor has on the table.

"No Set, No Bet":

Advice to fold on the flop if a pair does not improve to a three of a kind hand.

Nut Flush:

The best possible flush given the cards on board.

Nut Flush Draw:

A draw to the best possible flush given the cards on board.

Nut Straight:

The best possible straight given the cards on board.

Nut Straight Draw:

A draw to the best possible straight given the cards on board.

Nuts:

The best hand possible given the cards on board.

One Pair:

Hand containing two cards of the same rank, such as Q-Q or 7-7.

Online Poker:

Poker played on the Internet as opposed to "live" poker, in which players are actually seated together at a physical table.

Outs:

Cards that will improve a hand that is behind enough to be a likely winner.

Overbet:
   To make a bet that is greater than one and one-half the size of the pot.

Overcard:
   A hole card higher in rank than any board card. For example, a jack is an overcard to a flop of 10-6-2.

Overpair:
   A pair higher than any card on board.

Pocket Cards:
   The two face-down cards received by all players.

Pocket Rockets:
   Two aces as starting cards.

Position:
   A player's relative position to the player acting last in a poker round.

Pot:
   The sum total of all antes, blinds, and bets placed in the center of the table by players during a poker hand.

Potential Gain:
   The amount of chips that can potentially be won (assuming opponents will make additional bets) compared to the cost of a bet. Also Implied Odds.

Pot-Limit:
   Betting structure in which the largest bet can be no more than the current size of the pot.

Pot Odds:
   The amount of money in the pot compared to the cost of a bet. For example if 50 is in the pot, and a player needs to call a bet of 10 to play, he is getting pot odds of 5 to 1.

Pot-Sized Bet:
   A bet that is about the size of the pot.

Power Play:
> A hand that is believed to be inferior, but is played strongly by betting or raising in an attempt to drive opponents out of a pot.

Preflop:
> The first betting round in hold'em, when each player has only their two pocket cards.

Premium Starting Hands:
> One in a group of the best starting cards in hold'em: A-A, K-K, Q-Q, and A-K, and sometimes A-Q and J-J as well.

Prize Pool:
> The total amount of money in a tournament that will be awarded to the winners.

Raise:
> A wager that increases a previous bet.

Rake:
> The amount of money taking out of the pot by the house as its fee for running the game.

Rebuy:
> To purchase additional chips.

Rebuy Tournament:
> A tournament that allows players to purchase additional chips during the specified period of time, usually the first few rounds of play.

Reraise:
> To raise another player's raise.

Resteal:
> On the first betting round, to bluff a raiser who is attempting to steal the blinds out of a pot.

Ring Game:
> A cash game with a full table of players, usually seven or more.

HOLD'EM GLOSSARY

River:
> The fifth community card on board.

Round:
> See Level.

Royal Flush:
> An A-K-Q-J-10 of the same suit. The highest ranking hand in hold'em.

Satellite:
> One or two table mini-tournament.

Set:
> Three of a kind.

Shorthanded:
> A poker game played with seven players or less.

Short Stack:
> In a tournament, having less than ten times the big blind.

Showdown:
> The final act in a poker game, where remaining players reveal their hands to determine the winner of the pot.

Side Pot:
> A separate pot created for players who are still betting on a hand in which an active bettor has run out of chips.

Short-Handed:
> Poker played with less than the normal number of players, usually seven or fewer.

Short Stack:
> In a tournament, having less than ten times the size of the big blind bet.

Slowplay:
> To bet a strong hand weakly to disguise its strength and trap an opponent.

Small Blind:
> The smaller of two mandatory bets made by the player sitting immediately to the left of the dealer button position.

Small Pair:
> A pair of sevens or less.

Speculative Play:
> A hand believed to be a longshot to win, but because of its speculative nature, would hold surprise strength if the hand improves.

Standard Raise:
> A preflop raise of three times the big blind.

Steal the Blinds:
> On the first betting round, bluff opponents out of a pot no one has entered so that the blinds can be won.

Straight:
> A sequence of five consecutive cards of mixed suits, such as 4-5-6-7-8.

Straight Draw:
> Four cards in sequence needing one more card to form a straight.

Straight Flush:
> A sequence of five consecutive cards in the same suit, such as 8-9-10-J-Q all of spades.

String Bet:
> Additional chips added to a bet that has already been placed, which is disallowed.

Suited Connectors:
> Consecutive cards that are of the same suit, such as 9-10 of hearts.

Super Satellite:
> A low buy-in multiple table tournament that awards the top finishers with entry into a bigger buy-in event.

Table Bankroll:

The amount of money a player has on the table or has set aside for play.

Table Stakes:

A rule stating that a player's bet or call of a bet is limited to the amount of money he has on the table in front of him.

Tapped-Out:

A player who has no more funds from which to bet—he's broke.

Tells:

Body language, expressions, or mannerisms that reveal information about the strength of a player's hand.

Three of a Kind:

Poker hand containing three cards of the same rank, such as 4-4-4.

Tight Player:

A player who plays only premium hands and enters few pots.

Tight-Aggressive:

A style of player in which a player enters few pots but when he does, he bets and raises aggressively.

Total Bankroll:

The total amount of money a player has set aside as his gambling stake.

Tournament:

A competition in which players start with an equal number of chips and play until one player holds all them.

Tournament Chips:

Chips used specifically for tournaments and that have no cash value.

Tournament Director:

The supervisor responsible for organizing and running a tournament.

Trap:
> To induce a player to put more chips into a pot in which he is almost a sure loser.

Trips:
> Three of a kind.

Trouble Hands:
> Starting cards, such as A-J and K-Q, which can lose lots of chips by connecting with the flop by being outkicked or outpaired by bigger cards held by an opponent.

Turn:
> The fourth community card on board.

Two Pair:
> Poker hand containing two sets of two cards of the same rank, such as J-J-5-5.

Underbet:
> To make a bet that is one-third smaller than the size of the pot or less.

Under the Gun:
> The first player to act in a round of poker.

Washing:
> To randomly mix the cards on the table.

WPT:
> World Poker Tour.

WSOP:
> World Series of Poker.

GREAT CARDOZA POKER BOOKS
ADD THESE TO YOUR LIBRARY - ORDER NOW!

THE POKER TOURNAMENT FORMULA by Arnold Snyder. Start making money now in fast no-limit hold'em tournaments with these radical and never-before-published concepts and secrets for beating tournaments. You'll learn why cards don't matter as much as the dynamics of a tournament—your position, the size of your chip stack, who your opponents are, and above all, the structure. Poker tournaments offer one of the richest opportunities to come along in decades. Every so often, a book comes along that changes the way players attack a game and provides them with a big advantage over opponents. Gambling legend Arnold Snyder has written such a book. 368 pages, $19.95.

POKER TOURNAMENT FORMULA 2: Advanced Strategies for Big Money Tournaments by Arnold Snyder. Probably the greatest tournament poker book ever written, and the most controversial in the last decade, Snyder's revolutionary work debunks commonly (and falsely) held beliefs. Snyder reveals the power of chip utility—the real secret behind winning tournaments—and covers utility ranks, tournament structures, small- and long-ball strategies, patience factors, the impact of structures, crushing the Harringbots and other player types, tournament phases, and much more. Includes big sections on Tools, Strategies, and Tournament Phases. A must buy! 496 pages, $24.95.

HOW TO BEAT SIT-AND-GO POKER TOURNAMENTS by Neil Timothy. There is a lot of dead money up for grabs in the lower limit sit-and-gos and Neil Timothy shows you how to go and get it. The author, a professional player, shows you how to reach the last six places of lower limit sit-and-go tournaments four out of five times and then how to get in the money 25-35 percent of the time using his powerful, proven strategies. This book can turn a losing sit-and-go player into a winner, and a winner into a bigger winner. Also effective for the early and middle stages of one-table satellites.176 pages, $14.95.

DANIEL NEGREANU'S POWER HOLD'EM STRATEGY by Daniel Negreanu. This power-packed book on beating no-limit hold'em is one of the three most influential poker books ever written. Negreanu headlines a collection of young great players—Todd Brunson, David Williams, Erick Lindgren, Evelyn Ng and Paul Wasicka—who share their insider professional moves and winning secrets. You'll learn about short-handed and heads-up play, high-limit cash games, a powerful beginner's strategy to neutralize pro players, and how to mix up your play, bluff and win big pots. The centerpiece, however, is Negreanu's powerful and revolutionary small ball strategy. You'll learn how to play hold'em with cards you never would have played before—and with fantastic results. The preflop, flop, turn and river will never look the same again. A must-have! 520 pages, $34.95.

POKER WIZARDS by Warwick Dunnett. In the tradition of Super System, an exclusive collection of champions and superstars have been brought together to share their strategies, insights, and tactics for winning big money at poker, specifically no-limit hold'em tournaments. This is priceless advice from players who individually have each made millions of dollars in tournaments, and collectively, have won more than 20 WSOP bracelets, two WSOP main events, 100 major tournaments and $50 million in tournament winnings! Featuring Daniel Negreanu, Dan Harrington, Marcel Luske, Kathy Liebert, Mike Sexton, Mel Judah, Marc Salem, T.J Cloutier and Chris "Jesus" Ferguson. This must-read book is a goldmine for serious players, aspiring pros, and future champions! 352 pgs, $19.95.

HOLD'EM WISDOM FOR ALL PLAYERS by Daniel Negreanu. Superstar poker player Daniel Negreanu provides 50 easy-to-read and right-to-the-point hold'em strategy nuggets that will immediately make you a better player at cash games and tournaments. His wit and wisdom makes for great reading; even better, it makes for killer winning advice. Conversational, straightforward, and educational, this book covers topics as diverse as the top 10 rookie mistakes to bullying bullies and exploiting your table image. 176 pages, $14.95.

POWERFUL WINNING POKER SIMULATIONS
A MUST FOR SERIOUS PLAYERS WITH A COMPUTER!
IBM compatible CD ROM Win 95, 98, 2000, NT, ME, XP

These incredible full color poker simulations are the best method to improve your game. Computer opponents play like real players. All games let you set the limits and rake and have fully programmable players, plus stat tracking, and Hand Analyzer for starting hands. Mike Caro, the world's foremost poker theoretician says, "Amazing... a steal for under $500... get it, it's great." Includes free phone support. "Smart Advisor" gives expert advice for every play!

NEW!
Windows Versions
More Features!

1. TURBO TEXAS HOLD'EM FOR WINDOWS - $59.95. Choose which players, and how many (2-10) you want to play, create loose/tight games, and control check-raising, bluffing, position, sensitivity to pot odds, and more! Also, instant replay, pop-up odds, Professional Advisor keeps track of play statistics. Free bonus: Hold'em Hand Analyzer analyzes all 169 pocket hands in detail and their win rates under any conditions you set. Caro says this "hold'em software is the most powerful ever created." Great product!

2. TURBO SEVEN-CARD STUD FOR WINDOWS - $59.95. Create any conditions of play; choose number of players (2-8), bet amounts, fixed or spread limit, bring-in method, tight/loose conditions, position, reaction to board, number of dead cards, and stack deck to create special conditions. Features instant replay. Terrific stat reporting includes analysis of starting cards, 3-D bar charts, and graphs. Play interactively and run high speed simulation to test strategies. Hand Analyzer analyzes starting hands in detail. Wow!

3. TURBO OMAHA HIGH-LOW SPLIT FOR WINDOWS - $59.95. Specify any playing conditions; betting limits, number of raises, blind structures, button position, aggressiveness/ passiveness of opponents, number of players (2-10), types of hands dealt, blinds, position, board reaction, and specify flop, turn, and river cards! Choose opponents and use provided point count or create your own. Statistical reporting, instant replay, pop-up odds high speed simulation to test strategies, amazing Hand Analyzer, and much more!

4. TURBO OMAHA HIGH FOR WINDOWS - $59.95. Same features as above, but tailored for Omaha High only. Caro says program is "an electrifying research tool...it can clearly be worth thousands of dollars to any serious player. A must for Omaha High players.

5. TURBO 7 STUD 8 OR BETTER - $59.95. Brand new with all the features you expect from the Wilson Turbo products: the latest artificial intelligence, instant advice and exact odds, play versus 2-7 opponents, enhanced data charts that can be exported or printed, the ability to fold out of turn and immediately go to the next hand, ability to peek at opponents hand, optional warning mode that warns you if a play disagrees with the advisor, and automatic mode that runs up to 50 tests unattended. Tough computer players vary their styles for a great game.

6. TOURNAMENT TEXAS HOLD'EM - $39.95
Set-up for tournament practice and play, this realistic simulation pits you against celebrity look-alikes. Tons of options let you control tournament size with 10 to 300 entrants, select limits, ante, rake, blind structures, freezeouts, number of rebuys and competition level of opponents. Pop-up status report shows how you're doing vs. the competition. Save tournaments in progress to play again later. Additional feature allows quick folds on finished hands.

Order now at 1-800-577-WINS or go online to: www.cardozabooks.com